EXPLORING
MOUNT
RAINIER

Exploring
Mount Rainier

BY RUTH KIRK

Photographs by Ruth and Louis Kirk

UNIVERSITY OF WASHINGTON PRESS
Seattle and London

Bear cub

Title-page illustration: Mouth of Ice Caves

Photographs by Ruth and Louis Kirk, except: courtesy
U.S. Geological Survey, pp. 2 and 4; National Park
Service, p. 32 *(right)*; Curtis Collection, Washington
State Historical Society, pp. 38 and 46; Northwest
Collection, University of Washington, pp. 42, 50, and
56. Maps by Dee Molenaar. Flower drawings by Yoshi Nishihara

Portions of *Exploring Mount Rainier* have appeared in *Audubon Magazine*.

PREFACE

It was early May when we moved to Mount Rainier, which was to be our home for five years (my husband serving as district ranger). Spring mist veiled the mountain, and for three weeks we neither saw it nor knew precisely where to look. Then came the morning when the clouds lifted and the peak stood clear, white, huge—the sort of mountain that children instinctively draw.

Rainier is the fifth highest peak in the United States outside Alaska, and it soars above its immediate base more than any other in the forty-eight contiguous states. (The second greatest rise is Telescope Peak above the desolate salt floor of Death Valley, and curiously enough it was from Death Valley that we had moved to Rainier.) Part of Rainier's appeal is this lone rise: no other peaks shoulder it in a range. Part of the appeal, too, centers in the raw power implicit in a volcano: red rivers of rock during the period of building, and the ceaseless grind of glaciers after the cone has cooled.

My memory of living at Rainier centers, in part, on the spectacle of the mountain. We climbed to the summit—in a July blizzard, the first time; hiked the Wonderland Trail; and skied the unbroken midweek slopes while city folk were bound to their city tasks. My memory also is made up of small touches. We watched pioneer violets and calypso orchids bloom beyond our porch each spring, and awoke at night to the disputes of raccoons and spotted skunks sharing quarters under the house. We heard the chickarees scolding in the station's Douglas-firs and hemlocks; and we cherished the dappled fawns, the lone bear cub, the carpets of green oxalis and vanilla leaf in the forest, the purple and red and white of lupine and paintbrush and avalanche lily in the high meadows.

This book tells of both Rainiers—the mountain of grandeur and the mountain of myriad quiet beauties. Persons more numerous than space permits mentioning have made the writing possible, companions of road and trail, and experts consulted both in conversation and on the published page. To all, my gratitude and awareness of debt. And for the mountain itself . . . awe, and immense love.

RUTH KIRK

CONTENTS

Anemone seedheads

Natural History

GEOLOGY

THE VOLCANO TODAY

Mount Rainier floats on the skyline beyond Seattle and backdrops the harbor of Tacoma. It rises white and huge above Douglas-fir forests and fields of wildflowers and idyllic trout lakes. And the peace it evokes in the mind of the beholder stands in odd contrast to the fiery origin of the mountain— an "origin" that spread across millennia and is not yet done, for every indication is that the pace of geologic change is the same today as it always has been.

Several signs of the old heat remain at Rainier. Warm springs seep from the upper slopes, and steam issues from vents at the summit. A climber years ago reported that he boiled water in three minutes by setting the pot on the rock of the Columbia Crest crater, the 14,410-foot highpoint of Rainier; and a recent study team measured the ground temperature near the summit vents at 174 degrees F. (with a plummeting opposite of –23 degrees within the adjoining ice).

During the 1900's Puget Sound newspapers reported fourteen eruptions of the supposedly slumbering volcano, although no sure evidence establishes the truth of the accounts. They told of "smoke pouring over the highest peak" and of "steam rising from the mountain," but the observers were up to forty miles away, too far for accuracy. Probably the real origin of at least most of these "eruptions" lay in billowing clouds or in dust columns rising from rock avalanches on the mountain. Such dust still rises as tons of rock break loose and fall.

However, some newly identified specimens indicate that pumice evidently did erupt from Rainier's crater in the mid-1800's. Captain John C. Fremont noted in 1843 that Rainier was erupting, and there were eruptions of pumice between 1820 and 1854. During the same period Mount St. Helens repeatedly spewed ash over surrounding countryside as far as Rainier, but Rainier's own outfall was local, leaving only thin layers restricted to small areas with pieces of pumice often widely scattered.

Rainier's last major outburst was about two thousand years ago; but Rainier, although dormant, is not "dead." Lingering heat melts caves in the summit ice. One cave has 3,000 feet of continuous passage following the arc of the east crater rim, kept open by steam and ground heat; and temperatures of over 185 degrees F. have been recorded in the cave floor.

3

Aerial view of summit

Preceding illustration: Mount Rainier in winter

Summit crater from 19,000 feet

Now suppose, geologists say, that the molten rock within the core of Rainier were to rise even slightly. This would raise the temperature of the crater rocks, which could melt the ice plug of the crater, estimated as perhaps 500 feet thick and holding one billion gallons of water in frozen state. If the ice melted, the crater would hold a lake—which, incidentally, is how the summit of Rainier is described in Indian legends. If the rock rim of the crater should rupture, perhaps as a result of a steam explosion, the water of such a lake would sluice down the mountain, loosening clay and rock and creating a debris flow comparable to those that in the past have swept nearly to Puget Sound.

Whether—or when—such an outpouring will occur no one can say, but predictions have been made based on the type and rate of past occurrences. On this basis an eruption of lava flows from Mount Rainier is considered likely sometime within the next ten thousand years; an eruption of lava bombs within the next five thousand years; a pumice eruption within twenty-five hundred years; a steam explosion associated with a rise of magma within two thousand years; a steam explosion unrelated to a rise of magma within ten to one hundred years.

THE BEGINNINGS

The story of Rainier begins, of course, long before there was a volcanic cone. In that earliest time the area of Mount Rainier and the Cascade Range, just east of Rainier, was a coastal lowland laced by rivers and speckled with lakes. Through millions of years this land rose and fell, and the ocean alternately flooded inland to about where the Cascades are today and fell back farther west than the present coastline. This was the "Rainier" of about sixty million years ago (Eocene epoch), long before the mountain began to build.

The slow emergence and reflooding of the land lasted for perhaps twenty million years and produced the oldest of the four basic rock units that the Rainier volcano ultimately built upon: the Ohanapecosh, Stevens Ridge, Fifes Peak, and Tatoosh Pluton.

The Ohanapecosh formation underlies half of Mount Rainier National Park and much of the Cascades. It originated as molten rock pouring from volcanoes in late Eocene time. Some of the volcanoes were on land; the southernmost Cowlitz Chimney, near today's White River, is the hardened core of one such dry-land volcano. Most of the early cones, however, were submerged, with vents rising above the ocean surface just

Inside crater rim

enough to spew lava and debris into the air. Ash drifted five or ten miles before settling, and heavier material fell fairly directly onto the flanks of the underwater volcanoes. Mount Wow, near the beginning of the park's West Side Road, is formed of lava from these eruptions, shattered by sudden cooling in water.

Ohanapecosh rocks were folded, uplifted, and eroded. Then about forty million years ago, at the onset of Oligocene time, renewed volcanism began to deposit the Stevens Ridge Formation. Most of this rock originated as sheets of gas-charged ash that swept over the land and formed layers as thick as 350 feet, eventually totaling nearly 3,000 feet. These hot ash-flows devastated eighty square miles; the charred trunks of trees uprooted by them are still found swirled into the lower fifty feet of the flows.

The third major rock unit, the Fifes Peak Formation, dates from late Oligocene or early Miocene time, perhaps twenty-five million years ago. This rock has been eroded from most of the park area although it once must have been at least five thousand feet thick, judging from exposures in the Cascade Range. On the south side of Rainier, Fifes Peak rock is exposed at Unicorn Peak, and on the north it underlies Mowich Lake and Mother Mountain.

The last of the four "foundation" formations was an intrusion of magma, the Tatoosh Pluton. This molten rock was forced into the existing rock late in the Miocene epoch or at the beginning of the Pliocene, about twelve million years ago. On cooling, it formed an irregular body at least twenty miles across. Occasionally magma pushed explosively to the surface; few remnants of these outbreaks have withstood erosion, except for the Palisades in the northeast section of the park, cliffs of welded tuff 800 feet thick.

THE BEGINNING OF THE VOLCANO

Finally the great cone of Rainier started to build, rising about one million years ago from a rugged terrain with peaks already as high as 7,500 feet. The Cascade Range had been uplifted in Pliocene time and its canyons cut, forming a mature landscape with peaks and ridges and valleys. Remnants of this prevolcano topography are still evident at St. Elmo Pass, near Tokaloo Rock, and at Glacier Island.

Canyons as deep as 1,600 feet had been carved into the earlier formations, and lava from the first eruptions of the Rainier volcano flowed into these canyons, displacing the rivers. This caused the rivers to cut new channels along the edges of the flows and thereby reversed the topography. Gorges turned into ridges, and former ridges became the present-day river valleys. The ridges of Sunset and Klapatche parks are lava that filled the valleys of the ancestral Mowich and Puyallup rivers in this way, and Burroughs Mountain is formed of a lava flow that submerged the ancestral White River valley. A similar flow down a canyon resulted in the high

Andesite columns

tableland of Grand Park, located on the north flank of Mount Rainier.

Most of the early building of Rainier, at the onset of Pleistocene time, took place in massive outpourings following each other rapidly and layering one on top of another. The erupting magma was an andesite that cooled into various types of rock—black and glassy where it banked against canyon walls, and light gray where it was thick and therefore slower to cool; columnar at the bases and sides of flows, and in slabs and plates in the upper and middle portions.

Explosive showers of ash and pumice also helped to build Rainier, and lava mixed with snow started mudflows that further veneered the slopes. Most of these formations are neither extensive nor thick.

At about the same time that Rainier was actively building, the Cascade Range was buckling and uplifting, and volcanoes from Mount Baker to Lassen Peak were erupting. The entire Pacific Rim is dotted with volcanic cones along both sides of the ocean from the Aleutian Islands to Mount Erebus near the South Pole.

By the end of the Pleistocene epoch about ten thousand years ago, the top of Mount Rainier was at least one thousand feet higher than the present summit, and the total volume of the cone was nearly half again greater than it is now. The angles of the flows preserved on the upper slopes still point toward this previous height—especially the strata at Point Success, Gibraltar Rock, and along the ridge from Liberty Cap to Russell Cliff. Geologists once speculated that the top of the mountain blew off in a gigantic explosion, but the blocks of material that would have come from such an eruption are nowhere to be found. Recent study indicates that landsliding, perhaps set off by an explosion, carried away the summit area in a series of rock and mud avalanches.

One of these about five thousand years ago, the Osceola Mudflow, deluged from near the top of the mountain into the White River drainage, flowing five hundred feet deep in the valley near the present campground. Mud and rock inundated the sites of Enumclaw and Buckley seventy feet deep and may have flowed into Puget Sound lowlands as far as Auburn. The total of this one flow is estimated at nearly one half cubic mile. A similar mudflow started above Paradise at about the same time and poured down the Nisqually drainage, carrying material from the old summit and sluicing additional debris from the slopes it swept across. A later flow temporarily filled the Tahoma Creek and South Puyallup valleys with mud, spilling from one into the other by way of Round Pass.

Mudflows such as these, as well as pumice and ashfalls, continued to veneer Rainier until recent centuries. The last extensive eruption occurred about two thousand years ago. Pumice showered onto the entire eastern part of the park, forming a layer about six inches thick; and Columbia Crest, the lava cone that forms the summit today, built on the truncated rim of the old volcano. This outburst was only a few ticks of the clock into the geologic past, so recent that the summit cone is unflawed by erosion and the pumice still crunches underfoot.

THE GLACIERS

A volcano seems incongruous with glaciers—a juxtaposition of heat intense enough to melt rock with snowfall great enough to form ice. Yet, even before the Rainier volcano finished building, glaciers had formed and were sculpturing its lofty flanks.

Edmunds Glacier, looking toward Mount Adams

Crevasses, Cowlitz Glacier

Glaciers are the result not of arctic cold but of superabundant snowfall. Only two conditions are necessary for their formation: more snow must fall in winter than melts in summer, and this must continue over a sufficiently long period. Under these circumstances snow accumulates to such a great depth that it is compacted into ice and begins to move because of the plasticity of its lower layers. The crucial depth of snow varies from several tens of feet to two hundred or more, depending on the exact conditions and slope. Throughout the Pleistocene epoch, Rainier received vast quantities of moisture from the Pacific, borne by westerly winds and precipitated as snow. Ice thousands of feet thick radiated for forty miles from the summit crater and changed the mountain's silhouette from even-sided to deeply scoured. Sheer headwalls as high as three thousand feet formed as ice quarried the rock, prying and plucking boulders loose and carrying them downslope. Embedded rocks dragged against slopes, abrading; and the ice itself acted as a plow, churning whatever it crossed. The glaciers flowed down pre-existing V-shaped valleys cut by streams, broadening and deepening them, scouring and polishing.

About thirty-four square miles of ice mantle Rainier today, constituting the most accessible glaciers in the United States and one of the greatest single-peak glacier systems in the world. The Emmons Glacier, nearly five square miles in area, is the largest glacier in the nation outside Alaska; and several others are more than four miles long—the Carbon, Tahoma,

Winthrop, and Ingraham (with the Nisqually barely disqualified at 3.9 miles).

The exact number of glaciers at Mount Rainier is difficult to determine. The figure depends partly on the point at which ice ceases to be classed as a bona fide glacier and is considered merely a stagnant patch of ice, and also on whether an ice mass fed by more than one source but with a single terminus is considered a single glacier or a main glacier plus tributary. Most glaciologists list at least fifteen major glaciers and an additional ten to twenty-five lesser ones.

Active glaciers flow like rivers of ice. Movement builds enormous stresses as the ice conforms to irregularities of underlying slopes, and to accommodate to the stresses crevasses split the surface of the glacier. These crevasses are seldom deeper than one hundred feet because pressure within the ice tends to squeeze them shut beyond that depth. Surprisingly, the flow of a glacier is not that of a viscous fluid, like asphalt, but that of a solid. Ice follows the same laws of physics that govern the bending of iron, and is classified geologically as rock rather than liquid.

Within recent geologic time the glaciers at Rainier have been both larger and smaller than at present, reflecting changes in climate. Between fifteen thousand and twenty-five thousand years ago they were much larger, reaching six or eight times as far down their valleys as today. But for the last ten thousand years they have been essentially the same, expanding and shrinking in response to conditions but probably never disappearing entirely and never being substantially larger than at present.

Old reports for the Nisqually Glacier show annual recessions averaging sixty to eighty feet per year. This waning began about 1840, judging from tree-ring dating of the forest that followed in the glacier's wake. The corresponding date for the Emmons Glacier seems to be 1700, and trees on moraines of the Tahoma Glacier indicate a recession that began about 1835. The over-all pattern was a gradual lessening of Rainier's ice—and indeed all the glaciers of the world were believed to be melting back as the climate generally warmed and snowfall diminished.

In 1946 routine measuring of the Nisqually Glacier by the United States Geological Survey showed an increase in thickness at the 6,800-foot level, and the ice surface continued to rise in the following years. This "bulge" coursed down the glacier at a rate of a thousand feet per year, raising the total ice velocity from twenty to four hundred feet per year. This was the first sign anywhere of the change toward a cooler and wetter climate recognized as worldwide by the 1950's. A check of other glaciers revealed similar surges within the ice—a recording of a climatic change already underway that showed in the glaciers before it became apparent in meteorological observations.

The Nisqually and many other glaciers throughout the world began again to thrust forward, nourished by the accumulating ice of their upper reaches. The fronts lost the sagging concavity that characterizes receding glaciers and steepened into the convexity typical of advancing glaciers. Land previously relinquished began again to be covered by ice.

Advances were expected at the snouts of glaciers, as a result of the thickening ice, and in 1948 the Coleman Glacier on Mount Baker reversed its long-standing recession and pushed forward. Similar advances soon showed on many glaciers. The Nisqually terminus advanced in 1951 and has continued to elongate yearly.

The exact figures of an advance cannot always be pinpointed because rock overburden sometimes completely obscures the point at which a glacier ends. To cite representative figures, however, the Nisqually typically shows annual advances of 80 to 100 feet at present, the Emmons about 115 feet, and the Carbon 60 feet. For the time being all major glaciers on Mount Rainier are either advancing or stabilized. Many small ones continue to shrink.

Agents other than ice, some of them associated with glaciers, also shape Rainier. Water dribbling from melting ice and flowing in river torrents cuts the land, sweeps the silt along, and eventually redeposits it. Massive chunks of ice have occasionally blocked a drainage and backed up meltwater, then burst and sent the impounded water down-valley in devastating surges. The Kautz Creek flood of 1947 is a recent example.

Rockfall also alters the mountain—occasionally cataclysmically, as in 1963 when an avalanche of fourteen million cubic yards of rock fell from Little Tahoma in a slide that caromed down-canyon for four miles, carrying rocks the size of houses. Sheets of debris were borne on a cushion of air trapped beneath them, in somewhat the same way that air cushioned above a concrete rail "floats" an experimental train. The hurtling rock reached probable speeds of one hundred miles per hour, and perhaps of three hundred miles per hour.

Events of this type appear widespaced and sporadic, but their pace belongs to nature's infinity and not to the human time scale. Mount Rainier's future geologic pattern cannot be foretold in detail, but continuing change is certain; for change is the one constant that nature accepts.

Nisqually Valley

WEATHER

SNOW AND RAIN

Snow sets the weather theme at Mount Rainier: winter storms that last for days, and summer blizzards that whiten July meadows; snow that nourishes the glaciers; snow that by melting gives rise to the rivers, and by the pattern of its melt times the bloom of flowers.

Subalpine meadows at the five-thousand-foot level of the mountain, and above, are heavily blanketed each winter. An average of fifty feet of snow falls at Paradise from October through April, and 1971-72 brought nearly eighty-six feet, the heaviest snowfall ever officially recorded anywhere in the world. (In the United States, Thompson Pass, Alaska, has recorded eighty-one feet; Tamarack, California, and Crater Lake, Oregon, have each received close to fifty-seven feet in a single winter.)

By the end of winter the ground at Paradise (elevation 5,400 feet) is typically covered by 15 or 20 feet of snow, and one year the total depth had built to almost 30 feet by March. Rangers had to dig down into the second story of the ranger station, and Paradise Inn was buried to the dormer windows of its attic. Such winters grip the land into August, and some years the snow never melts from parts of the meadows.

Above Paradise the snowfall is probably even greater, but no one knows because winter conditions dissuade human observers and wreak havoc with automated recording devices. The increase must taper off toward the summit, however, because the air would be extremely cold and incapable of holding as much moisture as the air of the midslopes.

On the east side of the mountain, the meadows of Sunrise are essentially unvisited through the seven or eight months of high-country winter, but the snowfall probably measures only about half the amount at Paradise. Sunrise is almost one thousand feet higher but is on the lee side of the mountain and thus less vulnerable to the southwest winds that sweep storms in from the Pacific.

The low country of the park, such as Longmire (2,762 feet) or Ohanapecosh (1,914 feet), rarely accumulates more than six feet of snow on the ground, and two to four feet are more common. The rate of fall can be prodigious, however. Feathery, wet snow mantles every horizontal surface, swells twigs and telephone wires until they seem five inches

13

Subalpine fir in winter

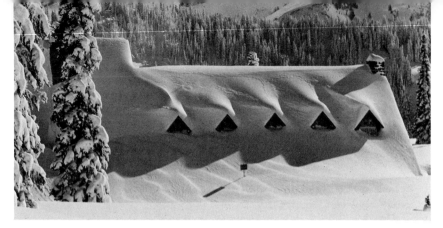

Paradise Inn

thick, and buries roads two feet deep between the time road crewmen stop plowing at night and the time they start again the next morning.

Trees become white plumes embossed against a white sky. The tracks of deer, fox, marten, weasels, snowshoe hares, and squirrels trace the path of their feeding into the snow, and occasionally the brush of a hawk's wings coupled with a track's abrupt ending marks the site of a winter meal.

Heavy, warm rains often mix with uncompacted snow in autumn and early winter, producing slush on the ground and swelling rivers disastrously. One such flood a few years ago ripped the concrete bridge from the banks of the Nisqually River above Longmire and swept it in chunks for ten miles downriver, prompting construction of the present bridge high above possible damage by flood.

Rain and snow combined average about one hundred inches of moisture per year at Paradise and eighty inches at Longmire. (Seattle's average precipitation is thirty-one inches, and Yakima's is a scant seven inches.) The sound of water is everywhere at Rainier—pattering against leaves, splashing from tires, roaring in rivers—and much of the year it seems that when it is not falling from the sky, it is rising back into the atmosphere from the saturated, steaming earth.

The dry season is July, August, and September. Thirty years of records average only four rainy days per month during July and August, and eight in September. Days are often simultaneously cloudy or foggy in the valleys and sunny in the high-country meadows. The cloudline on such days hangs between three thousand and six thousand feet, and visitors to Paradise either climb above the gloom or plunge more deeply into it, depending on the precise level. Conversely, the lowlands may be clear and the peak swaddled in mist, for Rainier makes its own weather. On these days mornings are more likely to be clear than afternoons.

TEMPERATURE

The Pacific Ocean moderates temperatures at the mountain the year around. (Puget Sound is only fifty miles to the west.) The ocean stays warmer than the land in winter and cooler in summer, and consequently air masses brought to Mount Rainier by the prevailing westerlies are warming in winter and cooling in summer.

The long-term January mean at Paradise is 26.8 degrees F. and at Longmire it is 30.0 degrees. Summer highs at Paradise typically register in the mid-sixties, and nighttime lows are in the forties. Longmire averages about 5 degrees warmer than Paradise. Bismarck, North Dakota, to pick an equivalent latitude, too far inland to be affected by the ocean, has a January mean of 9.4 degrees and a July mean of 72 degrees. Its snow depth averages about one foot during most of the winter, and total yearly precipitation is about fifteen inches.

SUMMIT WEATHER

Weather records from the summit are few—and distinctive because of the great elevation, nearly three miles high. Freezing is common as a summer maximum, and a research team camped at the summit once charted temperatures from –10 degrees up to 32 degrees as the complete range from May to September. Only one time that summer did the mercury climb above freezing. Wind blew incessantly, averaging thirty-five miles an hour and reaching one hundred. To escape it one team member slept each night for three weeks in a tunnel dug into the summit snow.

Such summers have prompted veteran Himalayan climbers to comment that Mount Rainier's upper weather exceeds the fury of anything they experienced on Mount Everest even at twice the elevation. However, most summers bring at least a little shirt-sleeve weather to the summit, and on those days climbers can rest and bask in nearly windless sunshine. Sunburn is a problem on any clear day, for no impurities filter the high-elevation sunshine, and the reflection from snow and ice is more intense than from sand and water at the beach.

Winter records for the summit are even fewer than summer records. Periodically, recording thermometers are installed, but the climbers who retrieve them report that they are insulated by as much as six inches of ice. Even so, minimums of –55 and –80 degrees have been recorded, and the actual temperatures must have been lower.

Cloudcaps may hug the summit of Rainier on essentially clear days, and lenticular clouds wisp to leeward. The peak thrusts above conditions that affect the lower air and therefore is independent of low-elevation weather. The summit soars high enough to disturb the flow of upper air, causing the condensation that forms the caps. Sometimes the cloudcaps are mere upper-air fog, persisting at the summit for days but not affecting surrounding weather. At other times they are the first sign of upper-air instability and foretell widespread cloudiness to come, for in weather, as in so much of its nature, Mount Rainier stands apart.

PLANTS

Plants in the meadows of Mount Rainier's high slopes grow under rigorous conditions. Soil is thin and rocky and tends to creep downhill, slipping over still frozen layers as moisture within it alternately freezes and thaws. Snow drifts deep in winter, and drought prevails in summer. Wind gusts to gale proportions and destroys the envelope of moist air that surrounds leaves, and thus desiccates the plants.

Temperatures fluctuate wildly throughout each day as well as throughout the year. This is especially true at the surface of the ground. Thermometers there may record a maximum of 110 degrees F. and a nighttime low of 35 degrees—a diurnal range of 75 degrees during a 24-hour period when above-ground temperatures are ranging less than half that much, from 70 to 40 degrees. The heat of the ground surface occasionally sears the stems of new shoots, girdling and killing them. Yet as little as 4 inches beneath the surface, temperatures hold steady at 35 to 40 degrees, presenting no difficulty for roots.

Winter often lasts until mid-June, allowing scant time for plants to complete their growing cycles before the next year's winter. Snow as such is not a problem—except to trees which it often overweights—but the early arrival of snow and its late melting reduce the growing season to mere weeks. During the winter, however, deep snow is actually an advantage for plants, protecting them from the frigid harshness of the subalpine world; their survival depends on its insulation. Of the plant species at Paradise, 85 per cent hold over their buds either barely within the soil or just above the surface. Without the protection of the snow these buds would freeze; yet their surface position gives a head start when the fleeting season for growth finally does begin.

ADAPTATIONS

Plants must adapt to mountain extremes. Animals can leave when winter comes or move to where conditions are less severe than the area as a whole; but plants must adapt in place—and they do, by shape and timing.

High country (and high latitude) plants hug the ground. Even trees are low compared to their counterparts in gentler environments. Some

17

Budding avalanche lily

willows mature when they are only an inch high, and along wind-swept upper ridges whitebark pines, Alaska cedars, and mountain hemlocks a century old may be no more than gnarled trunks three to six feet high, with flattened crowns that have been grotesquely shaped by wind. Among subalpine firs, low branches grow luxuriantly, protected by snow, and only tapering spires protrude into winter's ice and wind. The low branches often root, producing a wide "skirt" around the parent tree and eventually growing into a tight clump of trees or a ring bare in the middle after the original tree ages and dies. The process, termed "layering," is one of the main ways by which subalpine fir spreads.

Low growth is also important for herbs and grasses. The closer to the ground a plant grows, the less wind it is exposed to, since moving air drags against the friction of the earth and is slowed. Close-set stalks offer advantage, too, just as a grove of trees can withstand a windstorm better than lone individuals.

Cushion plants such as moss campion and phlox have additional growth adaptations. Their shape streamlines them against the ravages of wind, and their close-matted stalks hold enough of the day's heat to permit slow cooling at night instead of the sudden chilling experienced by single-stalk plants. The inner part of a moss campion may be twenty degrees warmer than the air—a temperature advantage and also an attraction to insects seeking shelter, which by their coming help to pollinate the plant. Furthermore, the cushion shape protects the plant on summer days by insulating the inner leaves and twigs from excessive heat.

In an experiment, plants were once moved from lowlands near the Tyrolean Alps to the upper slopes as a means of studying how survivors would adapt to a mountain environment. As expected, most of the plants

Phlox

died, but those that lived developed shorter stems, greener leaves, and brighter petals, and they bloomed earlier. Lowered growth had the effect of reducing exposure to wind and also of intensifying the utilization of warmth from the ground. Deepened pigmentation accelerated absorption of the sun's rays, which are already intense at high elevations because of the thin atmosphere. Life processes were speeded, increasing the plant's chance to leaf out, grow, flower, and seed within the fleeting time available.

Adaptations vary among subalpine species growing at Mount Rainier. Conifers and heather use the same leaves year after year instead of growing new ones. Subalpine lupine carries over rosettes of leaves through the winter, and as soon as the snow melts the plants begin to flower. Even so, five weeks pass before blossoms unfold, making this lupine a species that requires a site relinquished early by snow. Sedge and pussytoes, on the contrary, sprout and bloom quickly and therefore grow on late-melting sites.

Some plants at the six-thousand- to eight-thousand-foot level of Mount Rainier put out only two or three leaves per year and lengthen their stems only the merest fraction of an inch. These short-stemmed species often have proportionately long roots. A moss campion two inches tall may penetrate more than a foot underground. Its long roots function more to serve as anchor against wind and sliding soil than to thrust toward water, which tends to be near the surface.

Several plants bloom without waiting for snow to melt. Buttercups have been known to open their petals beneath ten feet of snow, drawing on starches stored during the previous season's growth. This permits a fast start on the new season, although the plants depend ultimately on sunshine for photosynthesis and the production of starches needed for growth and for the next year's reserve energy. No one yet knows what sets their internal clock for flowering, since the snow cuts them off from seasonal changes in light and temperature.

Spring beauty plants also start to sprout beneath snow, and avalanche lilies and glacier lilies are a common sight as they push up at the edge of snowbanks to bloom, their white and yellow petals following the melt pattern uphill, and replacing the white of the snow. Individual lily plants may bloom only once every five or six years: they need longer than a single season to absorb and store energy. If the leaves of these lilies are eaten by a grazing animal or picked by a human, the plant usually dies, lacking the energy to replace itself totally.

THE FORESTS

Twenty-seven species of trees mantle the park. They range from the wide-spaced subalpine trees to the dense lowland forests of conifers fringed with deciduous trees along river benches. The lowland forest lies like a

The evergreen mantle

deep-piled rug covering valleys and ridges from park boundaries to mountain meadows. The trees are chiefly Douglas-fir, western hemlock, and
redcedar. They tower taller than fifteen-story buildings—to nearly three
hundred feet—and their boles are commonly four or five feet in diameter
with occasional specimens eight or ten feet through. These giants are typically four hundred or five hundred years old.

Douglas-fir is not a true fir. Its Latin name formerly was *Pseudotsuga
taxifolia,* which means "false hemlock with yew leaves." (The name now
is *P. menziesii.*) True firs, genus *Abies,* intermix with Douglas-fir. Grand
fir grows along valley bottoms; silver and noble fir grow on slopes up to
the high meadows; subalpine fir grows in the meadows. Lodgepole pine,
yew, vine maple, and dogwood scatter among the lowland conifers, and red
alder, black cottonwood, and bigleaf maple canopy riverbanks.

Shrubs such as huckleberry and devil's club are also part of the lowland
forest, and so are ground species such as oxalis, vanilla leaf, bedstraw,
beadruby, twin flower, spring beauty, and dozens of others. Over one

hundred species of moss grow in the park, many of them forest mosses, and many others belonging to harsher environments. They are efficient "pioneers" from bare river bars to talus slopes. They lack the waterproof outer layer that characterizes the leaves of higher plants, and consequently they are able to dry and rehydrate readily as circumstances fluctuate. The pale green "moss" festooning lowland hemlocks and firs is actually goatsbeard lichen, a symbiotic combination of fungus and alga unrelated to moss. It grows epiphytically, using host trees for growing sites but not drawing nourishment or moisture from them. Instead, epiphytes sustain themselves with what washes down from above or comes on random air currents.

Swordfern, ladyfern, bracken, and deerfern form part of the green carpet of the forest floor, and licorice fern grows on branches of occasional maples and alders, much as goatsbeard lichen grows on conifers. About two hundred species of fungi growing in the forest have colorful fruiting bodies in fall, and the total species number over one thousand, including the inconspicuous decay fungi in logs and the myriad soil species. Fungus tissue soaks up water so quickly that the aboveground portion of the plant seems to spring up overnight. The strange fleshy flowers of ghost pipe, barber pole, pinedrops, and coral root are somewhat like fungi in that they also draw nutrients from decaying organic matter and seem to rise suddenly from the duff.

Ghost pipe   *Coltsfoot*

Above the 3,500- to 4,000-foot level of the mountain the forest begins to thin. Individual trees are smaller, the spacing between them is greater, and underbrush is sparse. From 4,500 to 6,000 feet the subalpine trees cluster in groves interspersed by flower meadows and heather slopes. Timberline is between 6,500 and 7,500 feet, depending on localized conditions. Stunted mountain hemlocks and Alaska cedars survive to this level, but no higher.

Herbs, sedges, and grasses continue to flourish wherever there is a pocket of snow-free soil, however, and lichens and mosses grow in the vents of the summit crater, kept warm and moist by steam. Plant life is so well adapted to extreme conditions that when an arch of the Paradise Ice Caves collapsed several years ago, exposing rock for the first time in centuries, seven kinds of plants invaded within six months although the nearest vegetation at the time of the collapse was a mile distant. Among the invaders were a lichen, an alga, two mosses, horsetail, grass, sedge, and monkeyflower.

Even snowfields can be a suitable environment for plant life. One type of alga lives its entire life cycle in snow, patching the white with microscopic crimson capsules in late summer and giving off the odor of ripe watermelon—but lacking the taste.

THE FLOWERING SEASON

Flowering begins in April when coltsfoot pushes up along roadsides and the yellow spathes of skunk cabbage color marshes. Trillium, oxalis, pioneer violet, calypso orchid, starflower, twin flower, foam flower, beadruby, and a host of others follow, stretching the season of forest bloom into midsummer.

Subalpine meadows usually stir to new life on the Sunrise side of the mountain by early June and by mid-June at Paradise. (There is less snow at Sunrise, and consequently flowering there both begins and ends earlier than at Paradise.) Avalanche lilies, glacier lilies, western anemones, and marsh marigolds—forerunners of massed color—herald the season in the high country. By July about forty species are blooming, even though snowbanks still patch swales and slopes: purple lupine, penstemon, Jacob's ladder, and aster; blue veronica; red paintbrush and columbine; white phlox, valerian, bistort, bear grass, saxifrage; yellow buttercup, cinquefoil, arnica, monkeyflower—and more, until finally blue gentian signals the end and the first snows fall, pressing down the vegetation, and the meadows begin to give off the pungent smell of silage.

By September huckleberry flames across the slopes and vine maple streaks avalanche runs with scarlet. Mountain ash and willow turn chrome yellow, the ash accented with red berries. The year comes full cycle; winter's silent white again claims the high meadows of Rainier and sifts through the trees of the lowland forests.

High-Country Flowers: White

PHLOX
Phlox diffusa
White flowers,
fading to pink;
ground-hugging mat

VALERIAN
Valeriana sitchensis
White or faintly
pink; 15"-20" high

AVALANCHE LILY
Erythronium montanum
Nodding white
blossoms with yellow
centers; 8"-10" high

ANEMONE
Anemone occidentalis
White, tinged with
blue; 6"-8" high, followed by
taller, shaggy seedheads

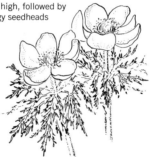

MARSH MARIGOLD
Caltha leptosepala
Often blooms in
flowing water;
white; 2"-6" high

BISTORT
Polygonum bistortoides
Grows upright, like
a miniature bottle
brush; white;
12"-20" high

BEAR GRASS
Xerophyllum tenax
Large ragged
clumps with flower
stalks 18"-30";
creamy white flowers

CASSIOPE
Cassiope mertensiana
Sometimes called white
heather; low mat

HELLEBORE
Veratrum eschscholtzii
Coarse leaves, flowers
greenish and
inconspicuous; matures
to 2'-3' high

High-Country Flowers: Yellow and Red

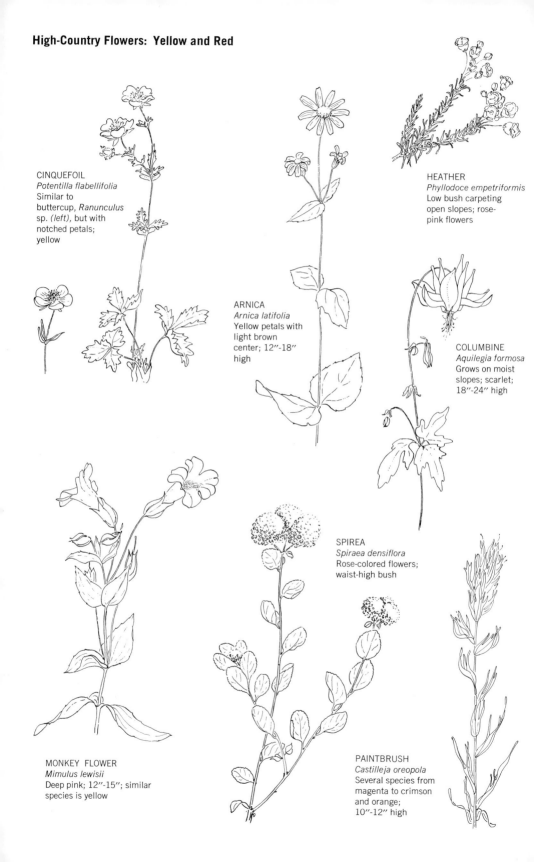

CINQUEFOIL
Potentilla flabellifolia
Similar to
buttercup, *Ranunculus*
sp. *(left)*, but with
notched petals;
yellow

ARNICA
Arnica latifolia
Yellow petals with
light brown
center; 12"-18"
high

HEATHER
Phyllodoce empetriformis
Low bush carpeting
open slopes; rose-
pink flowers

COLUMBINE
Aquilegia formosa
Grows on moist
slopes; scarlet;
18"-24" high

SPIREA
Spiraea densiflora
Rose-colored flowers;
waist-high bush

MONKEY FLOWER
Mimulus lewisii
Deep pink; 12"-15"; similar
species is yellow

PAINTBRUSH
Castilleja oreopola
Several species from
magenta to crimson
and orange;
10"-12" high

High-Country Flowers: Blue and Purple

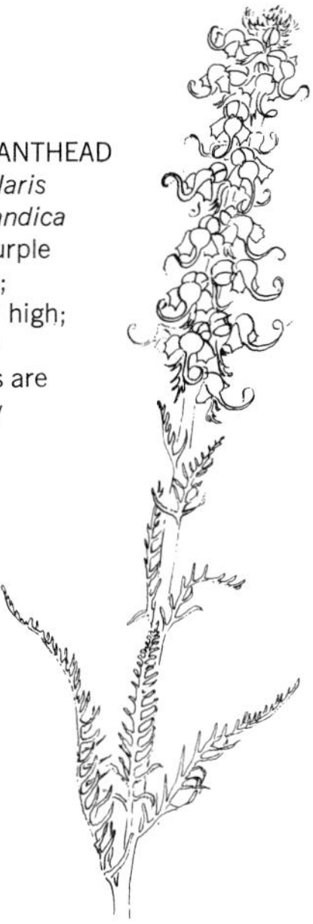

ELEPHANTHEAD
Pedicularis groenlandica
Pink-purple flowers; 8″-15″ high; similar species are creamy

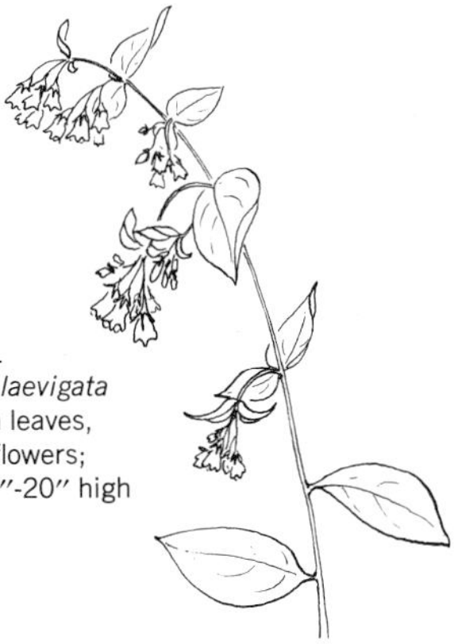

BLUEBELL
Mertensia laevigata
Pale green leaves, pale blue flowers; bushes 12″-20″ high

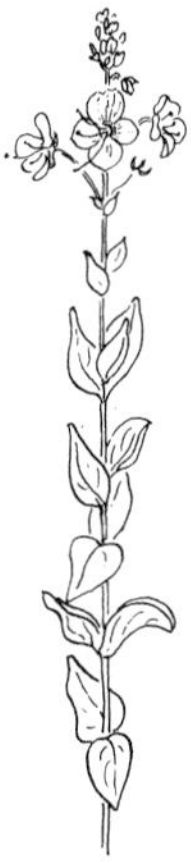

VERONICA
Veronica alpina
Also called speedwell; sky blue; 4″-6″ high

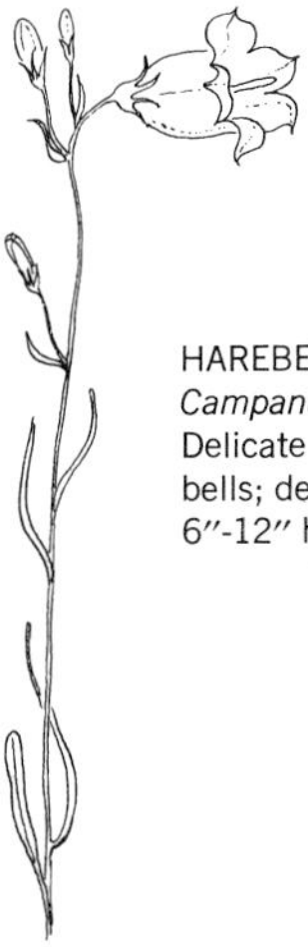

HAREBELL
Campanula rotundifolia
Delicate nodding bells; deep blue; 6″-12″ high

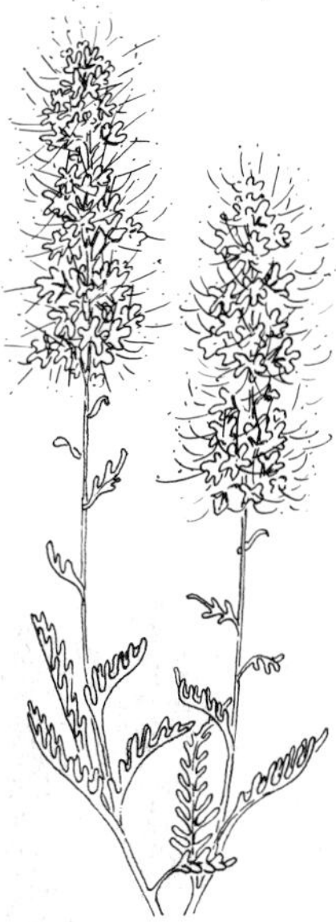

SILKY PHACELIA
Phacelia sericea
Purple; grows in feathery clumps, 8″-15″ high

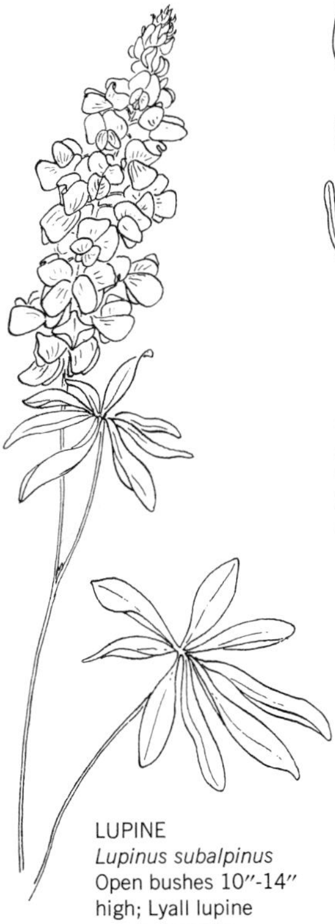

LUPINE
Lupinus subalpinus
Open bushes 10″-14″ high; Lyall lupine grows closer to ground, is smaller

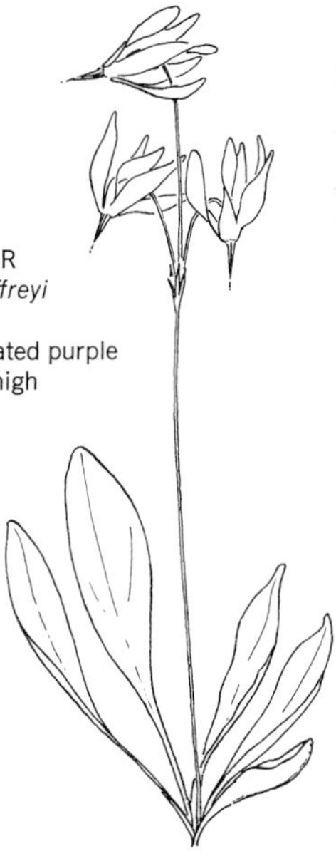

SHOOTING STAR
Dodecatheon jeffreyi
Grows in moist meadows; saturated purple color; 10″-12″ high

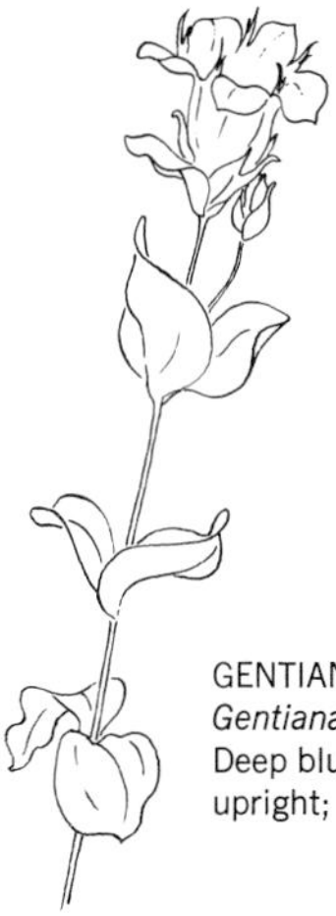

GENTIAN
Gentiana calycosa
Deep blue-purple; upright; 10″-14″ high

Forest Flowers

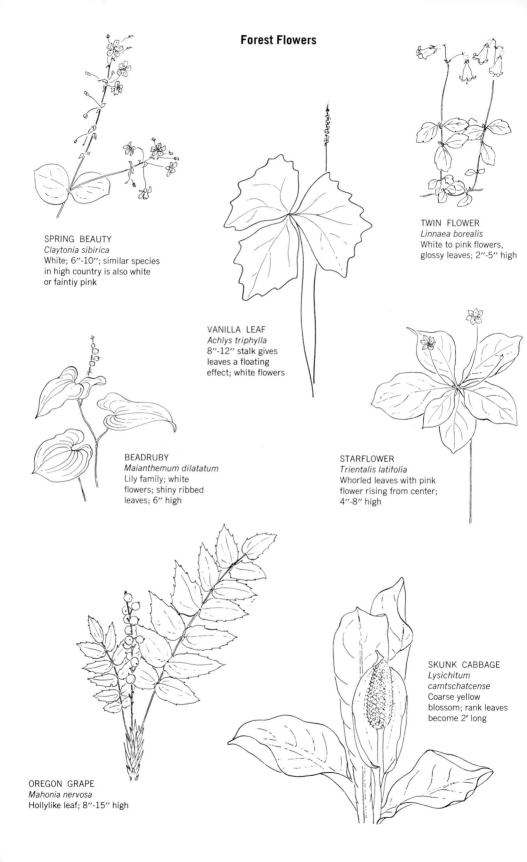

SPRING BEAUTY
Claytonia sibirica
White; 6"-10"; similar species
in high country is also white
or faintiy pink

VANILLA LEAF
Achlys triphylla
8"-12" stalk gives
leaves a floating
effect; white flowers

TWIN FLOWER
Linnaea borealis
White to pink flowers,
glossy leaves; 2"-5" high

BEADRUBY
Maianthemum dilatatum
Lily family; white
flowers; shiny ribbed
leaves; 6" high

STARFLOWER
Trientalis latifolia
Whorled leaves with pink
flower rising from center;
4"-8" high

SKUNK CABBAGE
Lysichitum camtschatcense
Coarse yellow
blossom; rank leaves
become 2' long

OREGON GRAPE
Mahonia nervosa
Hollylike leaf; 8"-15" high

Forest Flowers

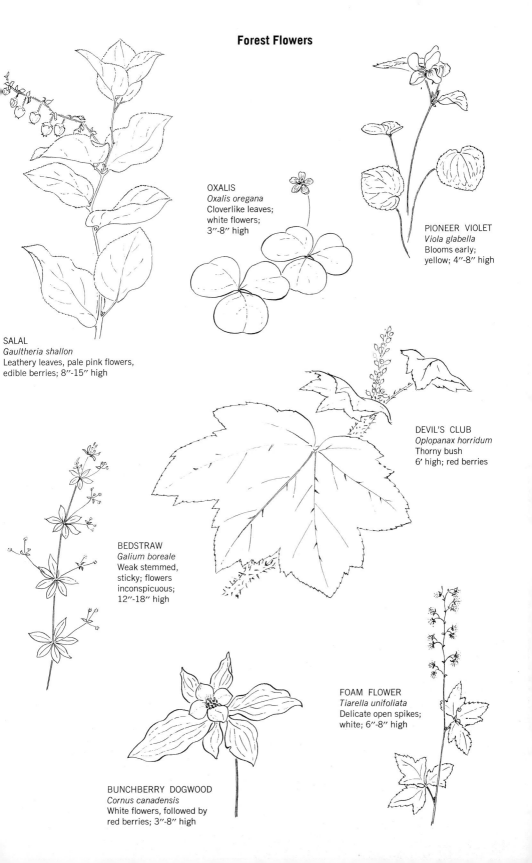

OXALIS
Oxalis oregana
Cloverlike leaves;
white flowers;
3"-8" high

PIONEER VIOLET
Viola glabella
Blooms early;
yellow; 4"-8" high

SALAL
Gaultheria shallon
Leathery leaves, pale pink flowers,
edible berries; 8"-15" high

DEVIL'S CLUB
Oplopanax horridum
Thorny bush
6' high; red berries

BEDSTRAW
Galium boreale
Weak stemmed,
sticky; flowers
inconspicuous;
12"-18" high

FOAM FLOWER
Tiarella unifoliata
Delicate open spikes;
white; 6"-8" high

BUNCHBERRY DOGWOOD
Cornus canadensis
White flowers, followed by
red berries; 3"-8" high

WILDLIFE

THE VARIETY

No part of Mount Rainier, from forest to meadows to summit, is without wildlife. A white-footed mouse was once seen running along the rocks of the crater rim, and pack rats and meadow mice wander as high as Camp Muir, at ten thousand feet. The high world of ice and snow differs radically from the "normal" environment below: there are no plants except for red algae patching the snow; there is blistering heat through the day and biting cold after dark; air is thin. Even so, animals make their way to the upper slopes. A porcupine has been reported on Disappointment Cleaver above Camp Muir, and Paradise hikers have watched bears on the Nisqually Glacier zigzagging and jumping to avoid crevasses.

Mammals on the park checklist total fifty species—bear, cougar, bobcat, elk, deer, mountain goats, marmots, squirrels and ground squirrels, raccoons, beaver, skunks. A few that once were here are gone. The timber wolf, lynx, and wolverine seem to have been extirpated from the area; fisher probably are also gone, and muskrat and otter, formerly common, are now rare.

Conversely, other species are increasing. One purpose of national parks is to preserve native animals in natural environments, to serve as "living museums" undisturbed by the human technology and commerical land uses that prevail outside park boundaries. But guns and traps often eliminate or greatly reduce predators and fur bearers before parks are established; or changes outside park boundaries affect balances within. For example, young growth on commercial forest land surrounding Rainier supplies abundant food for porcupines and probably accounts for their being more common than they originally were. Similarly, the reforested land abounds in rodents and rabbits—food for increasing numbers of coyotes and bobcats, especially since wolves no longer compete for the supply.

Changes also occur inside the park. People persist in feeding deer despite regulations and thereby encourage unnatural concentrations that result in the overbrowsing of small areas and the ultimate death of some animals by malnutrition when the season's handout ends. Ground squirrels and chipmunks are overabundant at Paradise and Sunrise because of human largesse; so are weasels to prey upon them. Bears panhandle by

29

Mountain goat

roadsides until rangers live-trap them and release them in remote parts of the park. Occasionally a bear learns to distinguish rangers from park visitors. Let a stiff-brimmed uniform hat intrude upon the vision of such a bear, and it will foreswear campground garbage cans and streak for the forest.

Mammals are only one type of wildlife in the park. Birds also inhabit the full range of Rainier environments, some of them at the higher elevations where they feed on clouds of insects that blow up from the lowlands. Trout and charr—both native fish and hatchery stock—swim in the rivers and lakes. Three species of garter snake and one rubber boa are here—all harmless, all eager to escape an approaching human, and all protected by park regulation. Alligator lizards, which are slow and unresponsive compared to desert lizards, creep about the forest floor. Amphibians include seven species of salamanders and newts and five of frogs and toads.

Ice worms and springtails, which spend their entire life cycle on and in the snowfields and glaciers, are the most surprising Rainier fauna. The worms are black, threadlike, and less than an inch long—shorter than their Latin name, *Mesenchytaeus solifugus* var. *rainierensis*. Sometimes only two or three worms are found together; sometimes the snow's surface wriggles with them for a square mile, eight or ten worms per square inch.

The springtails, black insects similar to fleas, also live in snow and ice. They are named for an appendage on the underside of the abdomen that releases abruptly and sets them leaping an inch or two, the equivalent of a jump of 150 feet for a man. Both worms and springtails evidently feed on algae and wind-blown pollen. Both find shelter in the minute crevices between crystals, and their dark color is thought to help them thaw their way in and out of the snow or ice by absorbing heat from the sun's rays.

HIGH-COUNTRY ADAPTATIONS

Heat and periodic drought pose problems for subalpine wildlife in summer, and storms often unleash their fury. But it is winter that is the truly hard time, with the severe cold and the difficulty of getting around and finding food in snow-shrouded terrain. Mountain mammals react in three main ways to the onset of winter: they migrate, hibernate, or carry on.

Deer are the most conspicuous migrators at Rainier, retreating from the high meadows to the protection of the dense forests when autumn snows start piling into winter's deep blanket. Elk, found primarily in the southeastern part of the park, feel the seasonal shift and move from the upper slopes to Ohanapecosh and forests outside the park. Coyotes also generally move down.

Many of the animals that stay in the high country through the winter now begin to hibernate—although like everything else in nature hibernation does not necessarily follow fixed patterns, nor does it induce the same

Marmot tunneling out of snow

effect in all hibernating species or individuals. Marmots may curl tight within their burrows as early as September, while days are still warm and foliage is plentiful; and half a year later they may tunnel up again although four or five feet of snow cover the promise of spring. Some bears continue to prowl after winter snows begin and even after denning up will interupt themselves to venture back into the world for a few hours or days. In fact, bears are considered semihibernators because they do not enter the deeply comatose state of true hibernation. Chipmunks are also semihibernators, occasionally resuming activity on sunny days.

Golden-mantled ground squirrels are true hibernators. They prepare a nest deep enough underground to protect them from the cold, and the overhead piling of snow adds insulation. The temperature in the nest typically stays at 45 or 50 degrees F. although the outside world may be far below freezing. The body temperature of a hibernating squirrel plummets from above 100 degrees to about 50 degrees, making the animal barely warmer than the burrow, so that it does not lose much heat to the nest. Heartbeat slows from three hundred per minute to one beat every twenty or thirty seconds; respiration falls from a count of two hundred per minute to four or less.

Hibernation is like sleep or anesthesia or a hypnotic trance—yet infinitely deeper, a distinct bio-rhythm. An animal needs only about one hundredth of its normal food supply during hibernation, an amount small enough to be supplied by stored fat. Glands operate differently during hibernation; hormones produce effects not duplicated in waking life.

Even more singular than the hibernators, in some ways, are the animals that endure the high-country winter with no adaptation beyond that of growing extra fur and perhaps changing from brown to white, as in the case of snowshoe hares and least weasels. Among the birds at Rainier,

Ptarmigan: summer and winter

ptarmigan also change from dark to white, complete with warm under-feathers and feathers on their feet to act as snowshoes.

Pikas, or conies, stay active in rock crannies under the snow, feeding on hay that they have cut and sun-cured during the summer. Their body temperature remains close to its normal 102 degrees, which means that the hay supply must provide energy for 6 or 8 months of undiminished metabolic activity with enough surplus energy to offset the heat that the animals radiate into the winter air. Meadow mice and pocket gophers burrow beneath the snow, feeding on roots and bulbs without regard for winter. In fact, the chief indication of them in summer is the winding ridges of earth that they have piled at the ground surface while tunneling beneath winter snow.

Snowshoe hares live in the surface world the year around, lifted each week by deepening snow to levels of browse previously beyond reach. Hunched motionless with ears back, legs drawn in tight, and fur fluffed, a hare minimizes the loss of body heat to the surrounding winter air; but when a fox appears it leaps for safety with a burst of energy that steps up its metabolism twenty times the rate at rest. This might bring on heat exhaustion except that by raising its ears it gives off heat to the air, and by stretching out to run it increases the amount of body surface exposed to the air, thus helping to dissipate the heat of the exercise. White-footed mice and martens also stay active above the snow—fortunately for the carnivores that depend on them as year-round food.

Mountain goats are the largest mammal to carry on through the Rainier winter without special adaptation or behavior. They remain on the high rock cliffs or shift slightly lower during lashing storms. These "goats" are not true goats. Antelopes are their closest North American relatives, and the chamois of the European Alps is closer still. Soft, slightly cupped hoof pads give mountain goats suction-cup traction for precipices, and when

Pika

succulent food is not to be found, their four stomachs can efficiently extract all possible nourishment from coarse browse such as fir and hemlock twigs or lichen. About the only adaptation for winter that mountain goats make is to grow a woolly undercoat and a shaggy outer coat, which hangs long enough to protect their lightly haired bellies.

WHERE TO WATCH FOR ANIMALS

Deer are likely to be seen from the forests up to the meadows during the warm months and in the lowlands through the winter. Most are blacktail, although mule deer—a variety of blacktail—are found in the eastern part of the park. Fawns are born in May and June; they should not be touched even if they seem to be abandoned. The doe almost surely is simply off feeding and will return.

Elk resemble deer but are larger, with darker necks and lighter rumps. The best place to watch for them is on Shriner Peak, an easy hike above Ohanapecosh. They graze the meadows of Shriner in herds of eighty to one hundred. Occasionally elk are seen along lower Stevens Canyon.

The number of bear in the park fluctuates enough to make them sometimes a nuisance and at other times almost a rarity. They may turn up anywhere during the spring to fall season. One summer a bear climbed the stairs of the Gobblers Knob fire lookout to the catwalk and startled the fire control aide by staring in the window!

Probably the easiest place to see goats close by is at Van Trump Park, a short hike near Paradise. Emerald Ridge and the Colonnades, beyond the West Side Road, and the Cowlitz Chimneys, on the east side of the park, are also favored by goats. They can often be seen with binoculars from the Paradise road on the cliffs across from Canyon Rim; or on Tum Tum and Cougar Rock near Longmire.

Marmots are found throughout the high country. Particularly good vantage points for seeing them are at Panorama Point on the Skyline Trail, along the road from Cayuse to Chinook Pass, or the Mowich Lake road. They sun on rocks or their burrow mounds, then scurry through a meadow to feed among bistort or lupine, holding the flowers squirrel-like in their front paws or ripping noisily at foliage with their teeth; or they may grub after roots, showering soil as they dig. When alarmed, they uttter shrill screams and disappear underground.

Pikas are another shrill whistler, but their cry is lighter than the marmot's, more of an "Ee-ee-ee" sound. The rock slides at Tipsoo Lake and in the Tatoosh Range are prime pika country.

Raccoons range throughout the lower forests; so do both spotted and striped skunks. Marten range up to timberline. Coyotes may be anywhere. Chickarees, or Douglas squirrels, stay in the deep forests; chipmunks and ground squirrels scurry throughout the subalpine country. Occasionally a female chipmunk will be seen shifting her babies to a new nest, carrying them one at a time with the loose belly skin of the baby gripped in her mouth, and its legs and tail curled around her neck like a fur ruff.

BIRDS

Of the 147 bird species and subspecies recorded for Mount Rainier, some seem out of place: Canada geese and pintail ducks passing through on migration; a double-crested cormorant swimming at Reflection Lake; California gulls standing on a gravel pile at Paradise, finding it the best "beach" available.

These are oddities, however. Most Rainier birds are in the area because parts of the mountain suit their needs. For example, the subalpine meadows in the northern and eastern parts of the park are ideal for goshawks, sharp-shins, and golden eagles, which need open country and the chance to see ground squirrels and meadow mice to prey upon. Robins and sparrows and finches feed on insects and seeds in the flower meadows; horned larks, pipits, sooty grouse, and ptarmigan seek higher and drier meadows and heather slopes. Their long legs are built chickenlike for running, and their tracks print the dust of trails and the mud of melting snowbanks in the alternating pattern of one-foot-then-the-other, instead of the both-at-once hopping of sparrows and other finches.

Olive-sided flycatchers and mountain bluebirds swoop from treetop lookouts to gulp insects on the wing. (Flycatchers can fly backward if their maneuvering calls for it, although unlike hummingbirds they can do so only momentarily.) Gray jays and Clark nutcrackers learn that campgrounds are promising food depots. Kingfishers and water ouzels follow rivers; the ouzel nests so close to white water that the young are splashed.

Woodpeckers and red-shafted flickers, mining tree trunks for grubs, break the hush of lowland forests with their hammering; creepers and red-breasted nuthatches also check bark crevices and tunnel for insects. Sapsuckers drill close-set rows of holes, then feed on the sap that collects and on the insects drawn to it to feed.

Golden-crowned kinglets and chestnut-backed chickadees flit through alder groves feeding on buds and insects; pine siskins and red crossbills rip open conifer cones; ravens and bald eagles glide along the river courses; winter wrens dart about the forest floor like feathered mice and alternately burst from the high tremolo of song into a scolding "chit," when disturbed.

The vignettes of Rainier bird life are many: a grouse dusting with four or five chicks in a bare spot between Paradise lupine and valerian; Vaux swifts and swallows streaking above the ridges of Stevens Canyon (the dive of a swift has been timed at two hundred miles per hour); band-tailed pigeons feeding drunkenly on fermenting huckleberries while coyotes patrol nearby; a redtail hawk circling overhead and panicking a marmot colony; a varied thrush calling in minor key from a thicket as daylight slips into dark, and the only other sounds are the roiling of the river and the snap of a twig as a deer beds down for the night.

Redtail hawk

The Human Story

INDIANS

THE TRIBES

As Indians along the west coast of Washington tell the story, Mount Rainier was once the wife of Mount Baker, or of Brothers Mountain according to the elders among Olympic Peninsula tribes. In both versions, this wife decided to leave her husband.

According to Lummi Indians she left because of jealousy of a second wife; and by Skokomish account she left because she ate so much and grew so fat that the Olympic peaks no longer had room for her. In any case, she packed her basket and set out for a new land, hoping at first that her husband would forbid her to go and then that he would call her back. She climbed the highest knolls and looked and looked homeward, but her husband gave no sign.

At last hope died. She climbed a final hill and scattered the flowers and berries and marmots and rivulets from her basket. She stretched tall in order to see her old home, and lifted her small son so that he too might see. And there wife and child remain today, apart from other peaks: Mount Rainier with Little Tahoma at her side.

Tribes throughout the lowlands were aware of the lone white cone, but there were no "Rainier Indians" living on the slopes of the mountain and calling it home. Len Longmire, early-day homesteader, reported that the Klickitat Indian name for the mountain was "Tahoma," pronounced with a short *a* and a long *o*. Other tribes used variations of the same word, and the meaning was rather simply, "The Mountain," with sometimes a hint of primacy—*Highest* Mountain, *Snowiest* Peak.

At the time the white settlers began arriving in western Washington Territory in the mid 1800's, parts of Rainier were claimed by five tribes: Muckleshoot, Yakima, Taidnapam, Nisqually, and Puyallup—clockwise around the mountain from White River on the northeast side. None had permanent villages within the boundaries of the present park, but all hunted at the mountain and gathered berries in late summer. The nearest year-round villages seem to have been at Eatonville, Packwood, and Rimrock, east of White Pass.

Land claims for an area as outlying as Rainier were not rigid, and intermarriage between tribes further eased proprietary feelings. Probably the Yakimas were the most seriously interested in the mountain as tribal

39

Early-day Yakima Indians

Preceding illustration: Nisqually Glacier

land. Fine horsemen, they traveled easily; and since their main territory lay in the relatively dry plains east of the Cascades, Rainier's lush forests and meadows offered valuable resources. The other four tribes lived along the rivers and traveled mostly by canoe, their orientation toward the ocean. Treks overland were out of the ordinary and difficult for them, and since they already lived in the forest Rainier's only additional resources were subalpine berries and mountain goats.

EARLY EVIDENCE

Traces of habitation are hard to find in the park. Where sites are not hidden by tangles of forest growth, they are buried by stream meanders and glacial outwash or churned by the frost heave of upland meadows. Caves or rock shelters would preserve records of the past, but Rainier's geology is wrong for there to be many of these. A projectile point about six thousand years old was found in a roadcut on the Stevens Canyon Road, and a small shelter beneath an overhanging rock was excavated near Summerland, above White River—the highest archeological site in Washington, at 5,300 feet. The shelter had been used for at least three hundred years and possibly as many as one thousand years, to judge by carbon-14 dating of charcoal from long-ago fires and by the style of a few stone knives and scrapers found buried in the floor.

The Northwest has been "home" for man at least through the last eleven thousand years, since the last ice age started giving way to a warming climate. At first the Cascade Range must have had no value to men because the mountain glaciers stayed active even though the great ice sheet from Canada had withdrawn. Furthermore, snowfields must have been immense and the summer runoff so formidable as to ring the peaks with mud and marsh.

Then, through centuries of warming and drying, the mountain became clothed with plants, and inhabited by animals, and, finally, accessible to man. By about eight thousand years ago the climate and probably also the flora and fauna were much the same in the Northwest as they are now. By six thousand years ago the warming had dried eastern Washington to a true desert, and primitive men were beginning to leave the valleys of the Columbia and Snake rivers and move to higher country, using the resources of the Cascades more heavily than at any other time before or since.

Next the climate reversed itself, and through centuries of cooling there was a down-slope retreat of the plants and animals and humans that had climbed during the long warming period. The cooling continued until the area became much colder than it is now, and then there was another reversal and a renewed warming. For the last twenty-five hundred years the climate has been much the same, fluctuating only slightly.

During these last several centuries Indians began coming to the sub-alpine meadows of Mount Rainier to pick berries, dig roots, collect medicinal herbs, and gather beargrass for baskets. Men hunted deer and elk and mountain goats, marmots and sooty grouse while they camped in the high country, but the women's harvesting work actually prompted the Indians' trips to Rainier. Huckleberry camps were set up each year at Indian Henrys, Rampart Ridge, Ricksecker Point, Paradise, Reflection Lakes, Sunset Park, Mowich Lake, and elsewhere—a tradition that continued with dwindling regularity into the 1950's. (Mount Adams is still the site of berry picking and sociability for Yakima Indians each summer.)

Women used to pick the berries into flat-bottomed baskets holding three or four quarts, and when these were full they dumped the berries onto drying racks spread with cedar or cattail mats. Poles held the mats high enough for a smoldering fire to dry the berries from underneath in case there was insufficient sunshine to convert them into raisins. Or sometimes the berries were poured onto mats laid on earth mounds close beside glowing embers.

When the berrying was finished, the Indians touched flame to the meadows to burn brush and tree seedlings that might otherwise encroach on the clearings. They rolled and hid their mats, dismantled their brush shelters and stored the framework poles. Then they packed their belongings along with the dried berries and dried meat and left the meadows, surrendering them for another year to autumn's dying foliage and the hibernating marmots.

Yakima Indians today, Mount Adams

DISCOVERY
AND EXPLORATION

FIRST OBSERVATIONS

Beginning with Juan Pérez in 1774, the Spanish discoverers who coasted Washington waters apparently did not see Mount Rainier; at least their logs do not mention the peak. Few of them entered the strait, however, and cloudy days must have been frequent then, as now.

Captain George Vancouver, the British seaman called the last of the discoverers and the first of the explorers because of his meticulous charting, seems to have been the first white man to be in a position to see the mountain on a day that happened to be clear. Vancouver came in 1792 to negotiate trade disputes with the Spanish at Nootka, on the west coast of Vancouver Island—an undertaking that resulted in the withdrawal of Spanish claims as far south as San Francisco.

En route to his rendezvous with the Spanish, Vancouver explored and mapped Puget Sound, and the page in his log for May 7, 1792, mentions "a remarkably high, round mountain covered with snow"—the first written notice of Mount Rainier.

The following day, rounding Marrowstone Point, Vancouver named the Peak: "The weather was serene and pleasant and the country continued to exhibit between us and the eastern snowy range the same luxuriant appearance . . . with the round snowy mountain now forming its southern extremity, and which, after my friend, Rear Admiral Peter Rainier, I distinguish by the name of Mount Rainier."

Rainier was the grandson of Huguenot refugees and the son of Peter Rainier of Sandwich, England. He served in the British Navy from the age of fifteen and was promoted in rank because of bravery in capturing an American privateer during the Revolutionary War—a point that rankled the patriotism of early citizens of Washington Territory!

Fourteen years after Vancouver's discovery, Lewis and Clark saw the peak. They had no direct association with Rainier, however; they merely recorded seeing it on their return trip up the Columbia River.

EARLY SURVEYS

In 1833 the British-owned Hudson's Bay Company established a waypoint for their men traveling from headquarters at Fort Vancouver on the Columbia to the company's next post at Fort Langley, at the mouth of

Mount Rainier, from an engraving in Captain George Vancouver's Voyage of Discovery

Nisqually House

the Fraser River. They picked a site near a small lake south of present-day Tacoma, and soon Nisqually House became an important pinpoint of civilization, the first settlement anywhere near Mount Rainier and the first on Puget Sound.

The same year that construction was begun a twenty-one-year-old Scottish doctor named William Tolmie arrived at the outpost, a man destined ultimately to become chief factor of the company. Mount Rainier towered white and lonely fifty miles east of the post, and Tolmie asked permission to trek to it. On August 27, 1833, he gleefully noted in his diary: "Have engaged two horses from [an Indian] living in that quarter, who came here tonight, and Lachalet is to be my guide. Told the Indians I am going to Mount Rainier to gather herbs of which to make medicine . . . part to be sent to Britain and part retained in case intermittent fever should visit us, when I will prescribe for the Indians."

Two days later Tolmie and five Indian men started for Rainier with the goal of exploring and collecting plants, not of making a summit climb. Lachalet had been hired "for a blanket," according to the diary, and his nephew "for ammunition." The Indians evidently expected to hunt elk and mountain goats for Tolmie records, "Lachalet has already been selling and promising the grease he is to get."

Food was simple. "Have supped on salal [berries]," a diary entry reads. "Had dried meat boiled in a cedar bark kettle for breakfast." "Supped on berries, which when heated with stones in a kettle, taste like lozenges." Once salmon were caught, and after breakfasting on them one of the Indians "stuck the gills and sound [guts] of the fish on a spit which stood before the fire, so that the next comer might know that salmon could be obtained there."

By the fifth day the men were close to their objective, and Tolmie climbed "a snowy peak immediately under Rainier"—probably Hessong Peak although Tolmie's name was mistakenly given to another peak. He collected plants from the high slopes and took bearings on a day that was clear "with every object distinctly perceived [and] Mount Rainier surpassingly splendid and magnificent."

In the years after Tolmie's venture, settlers in "North Oregon," by then numbering a thousand or more, started urging an overland route to Puget Sound. The United States government had sent an expedition under Captain Charles Wilkes in 1841 to cross the Cascades by Indian trail through Naches Pass, but the prime concern of the government had been the proposed United States–Canada boundary at the forty-ninth parallel, not a cross-mountain route.

The building of a road waited another ten years until a team led by Robert Bailey scouted a route through Naches Pass, and in 1853 emigrants managed to cross the Cascades by this route—among them James Longmire and his wife and four children, the sturdy pioneers who became the first to settle within the shadow of Mount Rainier.

Mount Rainier from Tolmie Peak

Saluskin, early-day guide

SUMMIT CLIMBS

THE FIRST TWO CLIMBS

The accounts of the first two ascents of Mount Rainier give no details. An 1852 newspaper item casually titled "Visit to Mt. Ranier [*sic*]" tells of Robert Bailey and companions climbing the mountain in connection with scouting a route through the Cascades. With Bailey were Sidney Ford, son of a pioneer family; John Edgar, a former Hudson's Bay Company shepherd; and Benjamin Shaw, veteran of Indian wars and owner of a Puget Sound lumber yard.

The report says little about the upper slopes of the mountain beyond commenting that the party "was two days in reaching their highest altitude" and had described Rainier as "extremely rugged and difficult of ascent." The four men seem to have climbed to about fourteen thousand feet, just short of the true summit, but high enough for their purpose of seeing "several passes at intervals through the mountains" to the east. They speculated that "a good route could be surveyed and a road cut . . . with . . . ease."

Two years later, in June, 1854, two men apparently climbed to the summit crater, but nothing was published about their ascent at the time, and their names and thoughts have been lost to history. Their guide was a Yakima Indian named Saluskin, not to be confused with Sluiskin, who guided later white men to Rainier. Sixty-two years after the climb the aging Yakima reminisced about it for the *Washington Historical Quarterly*.

Two "King George men" rode into the Yakimas' camp, according to the report, and introduced themselves as "Governor Stevens boys." They asked for a guide to Rainier, saying that they wanted to establish some of the lines set by recent treaties with the Indians.

"I look out and see them," Saluskin said; "both short, [not yet] middle age." One had "black eyes like an Indian," and the other was "tall, slender, not good looking, but about right [with] brown, not quite red hair on upper lip."

The sixth morning after starting from the Yakima camp for the "White Mountain," Saluskin saw the two men "put lunch in pockets and leave camp. I did not know where they go; but they start up the mountain. They put on shoes to walk on ice. No, not snow shoes; but shoes with nails in two places like this [touching heel and toe]. They start early at

47

daylight and come back at dark, same day. I staid in camp all day and think they fall in ice and die.

"The men told me they went on top of mountain and look with glass. . . . They said: 'We find lines.' . . . They said ice all over top, lake in center and smoke or steam coming out all around like sweat-house. Next day I went home and did not know where these men went. I left them there."

THE KAUTZ ATTEMPT

August Valentine Kautz, who was assigned to Fort Steilacoom—an American replacement of Nisqually House as the focal point of settlement—organized the third Rainier climbing expedition in 1857. "I was at that time a first-lieutenant, young and fond of visiting unexplored sections of the country, and possessed of a very prevailing passion for going to the tops of high places," Kautz wrote years afterward (1875) in the *Overland Monthly.*

He read about mountaineering techniques, then convinced an Indian named Wapowety, a doctor, and four soldiers to go with him to Rainier. The men fashioned alpenstocks and "sewed upon our shoes an extra sole [studded with nails] with the points broken off and the heads inside." They gathered together a fifty-foot rope, "a hatchet, a thermometer, plenty of hard biscuit and dried beef such as the Indians prepare"—and at that point Kautz judged their gear complete, their expedition ready.

At noon on July 8, 1857, the six men set out. "We calculated to be gone about six days," Kautz wrote. "Each [man] took a blanket, twenty-four crackers of hard bread, and about two pounds of dried beef. . . . Wapowety carried his rifle with which we hoped to procure some game. . . . We each had a haversack for our provisions, and a tin canteen for water."

The going was tough: "We often crossed the torrent [Nisqually River] of which the water was intensely cold, in order to avoid the obstructions of the forest. Sometimes, however, the stream was impassable, and then we often became so entangled in the thickets as almost to despair of further advance." But advance they did, managing about ten miles a day and commenting that "on good roads thirty miles would have wearied us less."

By July 13 they were climbing the Nisqually Glacier. "About noon the weather thickened," Kautz recounted. "Snow, sleet, and rain prevailed, and strong winds . . . almost blinded us. The surface of the glacier, becoming steeper, began to be intersected by immense crevasses crossing our path, often compelling us to travel several hundred yards to gain a few feet." The men clawed a way up the moraine and made camp in the meadows.

Next day the clouds lifted and the party headed for the summit, thinking the climb would take about three hours, but instead they found themselves still struggling upward at six o'clock that night. Kautz and one of the soldiers were the only two who persevered that far, the others having stopped lower down.

The two men reached "a comparatively flat place" where the going was easier (the saddle between Point Success and Columbia Crest), but a fierce wind and ice forming inside their canteen prompted Kautz to turn back just short of the final summit. He was already pressing luck to get off the ice before dark, and when the two arrived back at camp they found trouble waiting. The total provisions for the party were reduced to four crackers apiece, and Wapowety, their hunter, was snow blind. "The Indian needed our help to guide him . . . [his eyelids] were so swollen that he looked like he had been in a free fight and got the worst of it. He could not have told a deer from a stump the length of his little old rifle."

On the fourteenth day the party arrived back at Steilacoom. "We are not likely to have any competitors in this attempt to explore the summit of Mount Rainier," Kautz wrote, thinking of the difficulties. And then he added: "When the locomotive is heard in that region some day, when American enterprise has established an ice cream saloon at the foot of every glacier, and sherry cobblers may be had at 25¢ halfway up to the top of the mountain, attempts to ascend the snow peak will be quite frequent. But many a long year will pass away before roads are good enough to do what we did in the summer of 1857."

The climb had ended a few hundred feet short of the summit, but from the accounts of this climb the public for the first time gained detailed knowledge of Mount Rainier. The report of the Nisqually Glacier was the first notice of a glacier in the United States; and Kautz had also roughly confirmed a previous measurement of Rainier's height, the triangulation of 12,330 feet made by the Wilkes Expedition sixteen years earlier.

OVERNIGHT IN THE CRATER

In August, 1870, two climbers stood on the summit of Mount Rainier waving United States flags in triumph. There they placed a plaque bearing their two names, Hazard Stevens and Philemon Beecher Van Trump. Stevens was the son of Isaac Stevens, first governor of Washington Territory; Van Trump was the private secretary of a relative of the seventh governor.

A third adventurer had started with them, an Englishman named Edward Coleman who claimed to be an experienced Alps climber, but who actually proved an impediment from the start. He carried too much gear; he was too fastidious, and too easily tired. He struggled and lagged through the forest where there was a blazed trail to follow, and on the first day of cross-country climbing he turned back to wait at base camp.

The party had started from Olympia on August 8, accompanied by carriageloads of friends who gave them an all-night send-off party at Yelm. There the climbers were joined by a settler named James Longmire who

Hazard Stevens   *Philemon Beecher Van Trump*

had agreed to lead them to Bear Prairie, on the Nisqually River boundary of the present park, and to find an Indian who would guide them the rest of the way to Rainier.

The fourth day out, Longmire and Stevens went looking for the Indian guide. They had reached Bear Prairie and found the village Longmire knew about deserted, for the Indians had recently been forced to move to a reservation. A single family was living nearby, however, waiting for the huckleberry season, and here the men found Sluiskin. He agreed to act as guide. "Beside the lodge and quietly watching our approach" Stevens later wrote, ". . . stood a tall, slender Indian clad in buckskin shirt and leggings, with a striped woolen breech-clout, and a singular head garniture which gave him a fierce and martial appearance. This consisted of an old military cap, the visor thickly studded with brassheaded nails, while a large circular brass article, which might have been the top of an oil-lamp, was fastened upon the crown. Several eagle feathers stuck in the crown and strips of fur sewed upon its sides completed the edifice."

Longmire now started home, and the others turned toward Mount Rainier, led by Sluiskin. It was at this point that Coleman withdrew. Sluiskin had picked an up-and-down route that included climbing over the entire Tatoosh Range instead of following up the Nisqually Valley. Coleman threw down his pack and quit, going back to Bear Prairie. Perhaps Sluiskin chose this needlessly hard approach because he was being paid by the day and wanted to prolong the job, or he may have been testing the two Bostons and the King George man, as Americans and British were known in Chinook jargon. He believed it impossible to climb to the summit anyway. Sluiskin "deemed [our] intention . . . too absurd to deserve notice," Stevens remarked in his account of the venture published by the *Atlantic Monthly* (November, 1876).

After two days of toil the party made camp in the "enchanting emerald and flowery mead" of Mazama Ridge, and with Rainier towering close

Sluiskin at last realized that the summit was the men's goal. "In Chinook
. . . he began a solemn exhortation and warned against our rash project,"
Stevens wrote.

" 'Listen to me, my good friends. I must talk to you,' " Stevens quotes
Sluiskin as having said. " 'Your plan to climb Takhoma is all foolishness.
At first the way is easy, the task seems light. The broad snowfields over
which I have hunted the mountain goat offer an inviting path. But above
them you will have to climb over steep snowbanks and cross deep crevasses. . . . If you reach the great snowy dome, then a bitterly cold and
furious tempest will sweep you off into space like a withered leaf. . . .
Don't you go! You make my heart sick. . . .' ' "

And with that Sluiskin sat by the fire and began to chant a dirge while
Stevens and Van Trump wrapped in their blankets and tried to sleep.
"The dim, white, spectral mass towering so near, the roar of the torrents
below us, and the occasional thunder of avalanches . . . added to the weird
effect of Sluiskin's song," Stevens comments.

Next day the two men reconnoitered a route, and on August 17 they
started for the summit: "Besides our Alpine staffs and creepers, we
carried a long rope, and ice axes, a brass plate inscribed with our names,
our flags, a large canteen, and some luncheon. We were also provided with
gloves and green-goggles for snow blindness. . . . We left behind our coats
and blankets."

One of the flags the men carried had been specially sewn. Stevens had
cut the material and taken it to a friend who forgot to stitch the flag until
the day before the climbers were to leave. This happened to be a Sunday
—in an age when even light sewing on the Sabbath was considered a sin.
Consequently, Stevens' friend waited until midnight to pick up her needle,
and then because time was short she sewed on only thirteen stars, for the
original states, instead of the thirty-seven appropriate for the time. This
thirteen-star flag is now displayed at the Washington State Historical
Museum in Tacoma.

Curiously enough, the expedition's second flag was also short of a full
complement of stars. Stevens had borrowed it from a friend who came
west during the California gold rush, and the flag had only thirty-two stars,
eleven years outdated.

The two climbers expected to make a quick ascent and return to camp
by nightfall, but foreshortening of the mountain as seen from Paradise
misled them, and they underestimated the actual distance. Furthermore,
the going proved as hard as Sluiskin had predicted.

"We were now crawling along the face of the precipice almost in mid
air," Stevens wrote. "Several times during our progress showers of rocks
fell. . . . Mr. Van Trump was hit by a small [stone] and another struck his
staff from his hands. . . . We threw ourselves behind the [ice] pinnacles or

into cracks every seventy steps for rest and shelter against the bitter, piercing wind."

At last, however, the two men reached the top and "took out [the] flags and fastened them upon the Alpine staffs, and then, standing erect in the furious blast, waved them in triumph with three cheers."

Now a new problem arose. The day was even farther gone than it had been for Kautz, thirteen years earlier. Return to camp was impossible, yet death was certain if they spent the night exposed to the cold wind. Luck saved them. "Van Trump detected the odor of sulphur, and the next instant numerous jets of steam and smoke were observed issuing from the crevices of the rocks which formed the rim of the summit crater. Never was a discovery more welcome! Hastening forward, we . . . warmed our chilled and benumbed extremities over one of Pluto's fires [and decided] that here we would pass the night."

The men found a small cave melted out between ice and rocks by steam, and went inside. The heat close to the steam jet was too great to bear for more than an instant; yet their clothes, wet from the steam, froze stiff when they backed off. Furthermore, the sulphur fumes nauseated them.

Few nights could have been more miserable, but dawn came at last and with it a cloud cap that turned the summit into a swirling sea of wind and mist. At nine o'clock the men caught a glimpse of blue sky, crept from their cave, tucked the brass plate with their names and a canteen into a cleft, and began to descend. The mementos have never been found, not even by Van Trump or Stevens, each of whom climbed the mountain again in later years and searched in vain. Shifting ice evidently buried the two signs of the men's conquest, although they may yet reappear.

Sluiskin was waiting at Mazama Ridge when Stevens and Van Trump returned, but he had been about to leave for Olympia to report them dead. When the two men walked the last weary steps to camp Sluiskin at first thought they were ghosts; then he joyfully realized they were not and welcomed them with accolades of *"Skookum tilicum, skookum tumtum"*— "Strong men, stout hearts."

SUBSEQUENT ASCENTS

Two months after the ascent by Stevens and Van Trump, two government surveyors, Samuel Emmons and A. D. Wilson, climbed to the summit and made the first geological observations of the mountain. Within barely more than a decade Mount Rainier had thus been conquered as a vantage point from which to spy out surrounding country, as a satisfaction of man's urge toward high places, and in the name of science.

Successive years continued to bring climbers. Van Trump climbed a second time in 1883, and repeatedly in ensuing years. Longmire went to the summit at the age of sixty-five; John Muir climbed in 1888 and wrote poetic accounts that charmed readers and brought more climbers. In 1890 Fay Fuller, a Tacoma teacher and the daughter of a newspaper editor, became the first woman to climb Rainier. She wore an ankle-length "bloomer suit" of blue flannel and a long-sleeved blouse, but the costume was considered immodest in those days, and the public declared itself shocked at her unwomanly attire and behavior. In 1905, thirty-five years after his first climb, Stevens again stood on the summit—this time having arrived at base camp by train and automobile.

Today over two thousand persons successfully climb Rainier each year. Steel crampons made of the finest steel have replaced the extra soles studded with nails that Kautz devised, and lightweight ice axes take the place of the cumbersome old alpenstocks. Ropes are of nylon; food is freeze-dried chicken stew or scrambled eggs with ham instead of pilot biscuit and salal berries. Yet the mountain has not changed, nor has its basic appeal. It still demands physical stamina and mental determination of those who would climb to its summit, and while modern equipment has lessened the hazard and some of the work of the climb, it has not affected the spirit of adventure that draws men to the icy heights.

Climber today

Longmire homestead cabin

ESTABLISHING THE PARK

THE LONGMIRES

In 1853 the James Longmire family arrived in Washington Territory from Indiana. They homesteaded at Yelm, having been told by Hudson's Bay Company men not to take up land on the north side of the Nisqually River, still claimed by the company. A venturesome man, Longmire repeatedly probed the unknown wilds surrounding the homestead; he also served as a member of the first territorial legislature—the ideal combination of qualities needed for taming a frontier.

It was Longmire who guided Stevens and Van Trump to the base of Rainier in 1870, and who later that same year reluctantly accompanied Emmons and Wilson to their base camp at the mountain. In 1883, coming back from still another climb, on which he had accompanied the party clear to the summit, Longmire discovered the hot springs that bear his name. He filed a mineral claim and started to develop a spa.

During long hours and with aching backs, he and his sons improved the rude trail he had blazed years before from Yelm to Eatonville (then called Mashell Prairie) and on to Ashford (Succotash Valley). Tents began to blossom beneath the trees, and the Longmires recessed cedar tubs into several of the springs to accommodate bathers. The *Tacoma News* announced in 1884: "The springs, eight or ten in number, are a quarter of a mile from the river [Nisqually] . . . and within 25 miles of the glacier. . . . The Indians report cures being made from drinking the waters."

The Longmire family began to spend summers at their "Medicinal Springs" and winters at Yelm. They welcomed guests for eight dollars a week, the charge including board and use of the springs, which actually numbered about fifty, ranging in temperature from seventy-five to ninety degrees F.

"Longmire Springs presents a lively spectacle," Van Trump wrote in a letter to friends.". . . Carriages, buggies, carts, wagons are sheltered under the shade of the trees and many bicycles are in evidence, many ladies in bloomers, and others in various gradations and approaches to the full blown costume. . . . The peculiar garb of the wheelman contrasts strongly with that of the ordinary mountaineer; but everyone . . . is bound for that great Mecca of tourists, the great Tahoma."

55

The Indian name for the mountain was vociferously preferred by many—especially by residents of the city of Tacoma. Strident argument flared regarding the name of the peak and continued even after the matter was supposedly settled in 1890 with the official retention of the name Rainier, as bestowed by Vancouver a century earlier.

NATIONAL PARK

"Why go abroad when you may find Nature's own restoratives at your very doors?" asked an ad for the Longmire resort in the 1890's—and increasing numbers of vacationers evidently agreed.

"August 14," reads the diary of Mrs. Arthur Knight, a Tacoma woman who visited Rainier with friends in 1893. "Reached Longmire's and put up camp near one of the Springs. [This was the third day's travel from Tacoma.] We all took a bath in the Spring and felt quite rested.

"August 15: Got up rather late and made a trip to the glacier up the Nesqualie River bed, the glacier looked like a dirty snow bank until you

Mr. and Mrs. James Longmire

got close then you saw the clear ice with a cave underneath. . . . Got back to the Springs and after supper all took a bath. The water came to our necks and we were so light in the water that it took very little to support us.

"August 16: Stayed at the Springs all day and the women did some washing. . . . In the evening all went over to Mr. Longmire's and sang songs and had a fine time. . . ." And so on through August 28, including excursions to Eagle Peak, Paradise, and Gibraltar.

Tales of Rainier's grandeur began to ripple beyond the borders of Washington, sparked in part by a squabble at the 1893 Chicago World's Fair. A map drawn for the Washington State Building showed the mountain as "Mount Tacoma or Rainier." A public controversy arose from this renewed airing of the argument over name, with the result that the map was banished to an obscure back corner of the exhibit.

At the same time attention was drawn to the mountain capable of engendering such a stir. Scientists took note of the glaciers shown in early-day photographs of the peak and compared them to the ice of the Swiss Alps. Northwest newspapers pointed to the depredation at Paradise as campers hacked trees for firewood and bough beds, and even set groves of alpine fir ablaze for the skyrocketing brilliance of the display at night. It was time for real protection to be given the area, the editors urged; not just the paper protection of including the mountain within the Pacific Forest Reserve, which had been established the same year as the fair.

The Geological Society of America, the American Association for the Advancement of Science, and the National Geographic Society added their voices to the growing chorus advocating establishment of a national park. In 1899 Congress voted approval, and Mount Rainier became the nation's fifth national park.

The system was a new concept in the world: land set aside to be kept natural for all time and also to be available for the enjoyment of all the people, those living and those not yet born. The Longmires' land continued to be a focus of park activity; and administration centers and tent camps catered to visitors at Paradise, Indian Henrys, and Sunrise. In 1911 the road to Paradise was finished—although horses pulled the first automobile for the last few miles because of mud. President Taft was a passenger.

Today over one hundred miles of road and nearly three hundred miles of trail lace the park. Nearly two million people a year come to the mountain, almost forty thousand on a single summer day when warm skies canopy the flowers and the ice. Yet a short distance away from the crowd the essence of Rainier is unchanged: there is the same timeless grinding of the glaciers; the same annual ebb and flow of plant life, the birth and death of animal life. And people come to Rainier as they always have, to enjoy its beauty.

Enjoying the Park

TRIPS BY CAR

NISQUALLY TO PARADISE (Map 1)

Points of Interest: The road lifts from deep forest, past the snout of the Nisqually Glacier, to the summer wildflower meadows of Paradise.

Road: 19 miles; paved, gentle grades. See Directory for accommodations and services.

The forest inside the park has changed little in the century since Wapowety and Sluiskin led the early-day white men up the NISQUALLY VALLEY to Rainier—in fact, the monarchs of today's forest were already big trees when those first climbing parties walked beneath them. Douglas-fir and western hemlock, the dominant lowland trees, live five hundred years and more. They grow 250 feet high, yet root barely a yard deep. This leaves them vulnerable to windthrow, which accounts for the down trees at SUNSHINE POINT and TAHOMA FLAT, about a mile inside the park boundary. Fungus and bacteria will return the nutrients within these trees to the forest cycle, and many of the trunks will serve as seedbeds for oncoming generations of hemlock. Seedling hemlocks survive better in rotting wood than on the forest floor, largely because there is less competition with mosses and herbs. Douglas-fir seedlings however, require bare mineral soil.

TAHOMA CREEK carries a heavy load of "glacial flour," powdered rock ground from the mountain by glaciers and present in rivers that flow from active ice. A clear meltstream is one characteristic that distinguishes a "dead" glacier from an active one.

The scar of the KAUTZ MUDFLOW, 3 miles inside the park, marks the spent fury of a flood of sand and rock that swept the Kautz Valley in October, 1947. Rainfall was heavy at the time: almost six inches fell in a single day at Paradise. A torrent of runoff rushed into the already flooding Kautz drainage and cut through the glacier, collapsing blocks of ice and scooping out underlying debris. Water and ice and loose rock surged forward, became dammed, broke loose, surged again. Boulders later measured at thirteen feet rode the crest of the devastation, and trees up to three feet in diameter snapped through. Many of these broken trees are still standing, being exhumed as the creek washes away mud that is as deep as fifty feet. Also standing are trees that withstood the force of the flood but were killed by silt packing around their roots like cement and suffocating them.

61

New shoots of bracken fern

Preceding illustration: Avalanche lilies at Paradise

Kautz Mudflow of 1947   Tahoma Mudflow of 1967

A third kind of trees stands on the devastated site—the new forest. Within six months of the flood, new life had begun to tinge the raw gray alluvium with green, and now alder, cottonwood, and Douglas-fir are well on the way toward making the forest of tomorrow. In another century little but buried tree trunks and new layers of rock will mark the Kautz Mudflow, as is true also of countless other mudflows that have swept Rainier's flanks.

A nature trail leads through the mudflow devastation and the natural reforestation, about a half-hour walk. Guide leaflets are available at the roadside exhibit panel.

At LONGMIRE, 6 miles beyond Nisqually Entrance, one of the original homestead cabins stands in the meadow. Elcaine Longmire built this one in 1883, five years after his father had discovered hot mineral springs while trying to find his hobbled horses. The springs still bubble in the meadow. Mallard ducks sometimes nest in the reeds near them, and band-tailed pigeons flock in such numbers that the Longmire family named one of the springs Pigeon Springs. Occasionally songbirds are found dead near the springs, overcome by gases while feeding or drinking.

Today Longmire serves as park headquarters. Exhibits housed in a small visitor center briefly tell the story of Mount Rainier; open daily throughout the year. A half-mile, self-guiding nature trail (Trail of the Shadows) circles the meadow. Two trails lead to adjacent heights—Eagle Peak and Ramparts Ridge—but neither is recommended; they are steep and too forested to afford clear views. The same time and effort bring greater rewards by hiking trails that start higher or have more spectacular end goals. (See chapter on Hiking and Climbing.)

Above Longmire the road climbs past CHRISTINE FALLS (the highest part of the falls is below the road; park and look) and goes on to cross the Nisqually River by bridge about one mile below the snout of the NISQUALLY GLACIER. In the 1830's the ice reached down-canyon about fifteen hundred feet from the bridge site, and photographs of the first cars to drive to Paradise in 1911 show the glacier barely above the crossing. The glacier moves forward conveyor-belt style about eight inches a day. Rock overlays and discolors the lower ice, obscuring the true length of the glacier.

From RICKSECKER POINT (named for the engineer who surveyed the Paradise road) the view is of the Nisqually drainage. It stretches from the summit of Rainier where the glacier begins to the braided river channels disappearing into the lowland forest. The TATOOSH RANGE, ending abruptly in Eagle Peak, directly above Longmire, is formed of ancient lava and ash flows that predate the Rainier volcano by millions of years. The range is the southern end of a great U-shaped warping of strata—the Unicorn Syncline—that underlies Mount Rainier. The northern arm of the U reaches about three miles outside of the park beyond Carbon River.

The bare, dead trunks of the SILVER FOREST stand about a half mile beyond Ricksecker Point. They are remnants of a fire built in the late 1800's by the Longmires to destroy a nest of yellow jackets. Flames swept out of control through the underbrush and made torches of the subalpine fir branches, killing the trees but not consuming them.

NARADA FALLS, like Christine Falls, is best seen from below looking up. A short, easy trail leads down through the trees to a viewpoint. The water drops 168 feet, triple the height of Niagara Falls.

Summer flowers are the great "show" at PARADISE, an outpouring of renewed life that patches the slopes with wave after wave of color from the first white of avalanche lilies in late June or July to the September blue of gentian. The flowers prompted the name "Paradise." Mrs. James Longmire was so enchanted by them on her first visit that she exclaimed, "Why this is just like Paradise." And so it seems—as long as the weather is mild. In other moods the area is a white hell of driving snow needles and pelting flakes; or merely an endless, blinding sea of gray fog and drizzle.

The Paradise Visitor Center offers exhibits and illustrated programs, and ranger-naturalists lead walks during the summer. Check current schedules. In winter the area is open for skiing, snowshoeing, and sliding; ski tows (rope and Pomalift) and meal service operate on weekends and holidays only.

Be sure at least to sample the trails at Paradise; the beauty is only hinted at through the windshield of a moving car. (See Map 1 and also detailed trail sketch at back of book; also Hiking chapter. See Directory for accommodations.)

STEVENS CANYON (Map 2)

Points of Interest: The road crosses a lake-dotted bench, then cuts along the sheer face of Stevens Ridge, around the forested slope of Backbone Ridge, and down to Ohanapecosh.

Road: 23 miles; paved. Closed in winter, usually mid-October to June. No accommodations or services; campground at Ohanapecosh.

REFLECTION LAKE and LAKE LOUISE are cupped in the hummocky wake of the Paradise Mudflow, which four or five thousand years ago veneered everything in its path from near the mountain summit to Tahoma Creek. On clear, still days Reflection Lake mirrors Rainier perfectly, and at dusk trout dimple the image as they rise to feed. Listen for pikas in the talus above the lake and watch for calliope hummingbirds. This is the smallest bird in the United States, but with such proportionately large wings that if scaled up to swan-size the bird's wingspan would be thirty-two feet. The usual summer range of this hummer is the hot, dry country east of the Cascades; hence at Rainier it prefers the dry slopes of Stevens Canyon, the hottest in the park.

The Reflection Lake area is idyllic in fall, when slopes and lakeshores glow yellow and red with mountain ash and huckleberry, and the huckleberries are ripe for picking—by both humans and bears. The Pinnacle Peak trail leaves from the Reflection Lake parking area; the Bench and Snow lakes trailhead is about 2 miles beyond. (See Hiking chapter.)

STEVENS CANYON stretches directly ahead as the road rounds a horseshoe curve 2 miles beyond Reflection Lake. The U shape of the canyon is plain, a classic sign of glaciation. Ice alone does not carve this type of canyon, but by flowing in an established stream channel it deepens and broadens a pre-existing valley. Avalanche runs gouge the walls of Stevens Canyon where tons of snow and rock plunge from the ridgetop to the canyon floor each winter. Huckleberry and mountain ash grow on the lower spills of some of the runs, and subalpine fir stripes them higher up.

At BOX CANYON, 11 miles from Paradise, the Cowlitz River has cut into an ancient lava flow eroding a gorge 115 feet deep and only 13 feet wide at one point. A display explains the geology of the canyon, and a trail on the opposite side of the road crosses the narrow throat of the canyon by footbridge, then loops back to the road through the forest, a ten-minute walk. The bare rock, rounded and smooth, was polished by ice that inched down the mountain for centuries before melting back three or four hundred years ago. Lichens, mosses, and grasses are beginning the long cycle of revegetation of the rock, growing in cracks; a few seedlings of Douglas-fir, white pine, and Alaska cedar have also found enough soil to sustain life although they grow exceedingly slowly.

The volcano on the far horizon as seen from Box Canyon is Mount Adams, 40 miles south of Mount Rainier.

Crossing BACKBONE RIDGE the road offers a last view back to Rainier before dropping into the dense forest of Ohanapecosh. Unicorn Peak, the high point of the Tatoosh Range, dominates the skyline close by. Its 6,939-foot elevation and craggy bulk would make Unicorn an imposing peak if it were not overwhelmed by Mount Rainier, which dwarfs all else.

Box Canyon

OHANAPECOSH TO SUNRISE (Maps 3 and 4)

Points of Interest: The road threads the valley of the Ohanapecosh River; then climbs Cayuse Pass, drops to White River, and switchbacks up Sunrise Ridge to end amid subalpine meadows and sweeping panoramas.

Road: 33 miles; paved, easy grades. The north-south road, State 410, is open in winter except during severe snowstorms or periods of avalanching; Chinook Pass and Sunrise roads are closed by snow through the winter. See Directory for services available.

Sixty square miles of the park are forested, and some of the most impressive stands are in the OHANAPECOSH area. A visitor center introduces features of the forest, and ranger-naturalists lead short hikes in summer. Campfire programs are held nightly from July to Labor Day. A bubbling hot spring with water up to 124 degrees F. is accessible from the campground. A bathhouse formerly stood near the spring. (No accommodations now other than the campground; see Directory for nearest hostelries.)

The word "Ohanapecosh" is Indian, meaning "clear water"—an apt name for this river (good fishing; flies only). The hour-and-a-half loop walk to Silver Falls introduces both forest and river; or follow the ten-minute spur trail from the highway. Notice the deep slot of the box canyon just below the falls, and the vantage points overlooking the thundering water—some of them close enough to feel the spray and to find huckleberry and thimbleberry jeweled with droplets. Upriver from Silver Falls, the Trail of the Patriarchs winds through a cathedral grove of redcedars ten feet in diameter and perhaps five or six hundred years old. Douglas-fir and western hemlock intersperse with the cedar, and seedlings turn fallen trees into shaggy "nurselogs." The trail begins at the upper end of the parking lot by Stevens Canyon Entrance Station (allow forty-five minutes); or hike to the big trees from Silver Falls, about a mile. See Hiking chapter; also map and trail sketch at back of book.

Beyond Ohanapecosh the road rises along the east wall of a forested valley to cross the saddle of CAYUSE PASS (4,675 feet) and then drops to the White River Valley. CHINOOK PASS turns east from Cayuse Pass, a side trip of 3 miles to the crest of the Cascade Mountains (5,400 feet at the pass). From there it continues out of the park and on to Yakima.

TIPSOO LAKE lies pocketed on the subalpine slopes of Yakima Peak, just below Chinook Pass. It is small—only eight acres—but ringed with flowers during the fleeting snow-free weeks and backdropped by the vastness of Mount Rainier. The path worn into the sward at the lake shore points to the problem of scenic spots being simultaneously admired and marred—"loved to death," as someone has termed it. Trampling threatens permanent damage especially on hillsides where water from melting snow gullies human paths into serious erosion. This is the dilemma of increased use of wild country, which rightfully is open to all and yet is too fragile to withstand mass impact. Regulation—"planned sharing"—seems to be the only answer, however antithetical it is to the sense of freedom that draws men to open country.

For a sweeping view of the forested valleys of Rainier and the ice-clad cone soaring above them, walk to the Dewey Lake overlook. The trail begins across the road from Tipsoo; allow an hour, round trip.

The name of the WHITE RIVER comes from the glacial flour it carries from the Emmons Glacier. Notice the braid pattern of the river's channel, as seen from vantage points along the road to Sunrise. Glacier-fed rivers characteristically wander across rubble-strewn beds this way, changing course, dividing into separate channels, reuniting. The flow of the White River fluctuates widely depending on the amount of meltwater from the glacier. On summer days it may flow about one hundred cubic feet per second in the morning, then quicken to seven hundred cubic feet per second during the heat of midafternoon. With this surge, the water reoccupies old channels and picks up more gravel and rock than it can carry far. This load is redeposited, and a new channel is scoured around the obstruction, thus forming the braid pattern.

About 8 miles past where the Sunrise road branches off State 410, notice the outcropping of rock "columns"—lava (andesite) that flowed from the vents of the growing Rainier volcano and cooled rapidly, forming generally six-sided columns. About 2 miles farther, at Sunrise Point, the light gray granodiorite of the Tatoosh Pluton shows plainly, the upwelling of magma that underlies Mount Rainier and much of the Cascades, and is older than the columnar andesite formation.

SUNRISE POINT provides one of the most sweeping roadside views in the park. Five volcanoes are visible: the huge bulk of Mount Rainier close by, Glacier Peak and Mount Baker to the north, Mount Hood and Mount Adams to the south. There are eleven volcanic cones of ten thousand feet or over between Mount Baker and Lassen Peak in California, and uncounted scores of lesser ones. These all formed at about the same time, beginning roughly thirty million years ago. Rainier is the highest, 14,410 feet. Baker is 10,750 feet; Glacier, 10,541; Hood, 11,245; and Adams, 12,307. Mount Garibaldi, northeast of Vancouver, British Columbia, is also volcanic, 8,787 feet.

The SUNRISE area (formerly called YAKIMA PARK) is a stair-stepping ridge that juts from Mount Rainier for about 3 miles. The soil is mostly pumice that issued as molten rock from volcanic eruptions and was carried here by wind. Some of the pumice came from explosions of Mount Rainier, some from Mount St. Helens and from Mount Mazama (Crater Lake, in Oregon). Pumice fragments as large as one foot in diameter have been found on Goat Island Mountain, although the usual sizes are from one to four inches. Some of the pumice from Mount St. Helens still holds hairlike filaments of glass within it.

Grasses are more conspicuous at Sunrise than at Paradise, because of drier conditions, and the variety of flowers is slightly less—although the difference is scarcely noticeable. The dominant trees are subalpine fir, but mountain hemlock and whitebark pine are also common. The most nearly

Sunrise

alpine of the pines, whitebark grows at elevations no lower than five thousand feet at Rainier and survives on rocky crests up to seventy-five hundred feet where wind is incessant and soil scant.

Displays in the Sunrise Visitor Center tell the story of Mount Rainier's geology and botany; ranger-naturalists lead walks through the flower meadows during summer. (See Directory for accommodations and services.)

One of the best flower trails from the time the snow melts in late June or July through September is the Sourdough Mountain trail. Sample it a short way, or walk the 2 or 3 miles down the ridge to Sunrise Point and be met by car. (See Map 4 and trail sketch at back of book; also Hiking chapter.)

To see the glacier, walk the Emmons Vista trail which starts at the south side of the parking plaza near the beginning of the lower campground road. Allow twenty or thirty minutes, round trip, to the overlook and exhibits reached by turning left at the first trail junction; or turn right and walk along the canyon rim for a continuing view of the Emmons Glacier sweeping from summit-fed icefields, sixty-four hundred feet above, to the winding thread of the White River, eighteen hundred feet below. Much of the valley floor and the lower glacier is covered one hundred feet thick with debris that fell from Little Tahoma in 1963 in a series of rock avalanches totaling fourteen million cubic yards. Few views of Mount Rainier are as dramatic as this one. The distance is enough to permit a full view, yet close enough for the great crevasses that split the ice to be seen and for the continual roar of the river to be heard. The sights and sounds are of landscape in the making—not already formed, but still forming.

Mowich Lake

CARBON RIVER AND MOWICH LAKE (Map 5)

Points of Interest: Deep forest at Carbon River; lake, meadows, and hikes at Mowich.

Road: 14 miles by narrow paved road from the town of Wilkeson to Carbon River entrance of the park; then 5 miles, mostly unpaved to end of road; often closed in winter. The Mowich Lake road turns off 6.3 miles from Wilkeson. Unpaved; closed in winter; may soon dead-end in about 15 miles, leaving the lake accessible only by trail. Camping at Carbon River or the end of the Mowich road; no other facilities or services.

CARBON RIVER was named because of coal deposits that formed about fifty million years ago as the sands and muds of the primordial Rainier area solidified into sandstone and shale, compressing accumulations of plant material. The seams are thin compared to those of eastern United States, but they served Washington during the settlement period. In 1873 the railroad reached Tacoma from the Columbia River, and it was expected that men would soon lay steel eastward over the Cascade Range to join the mainline at the Snake River. Financial trouble delayed the start, however, and when work finally began the track was laid to the newly discovered coal fields instead of across the mountains. Wilkeson and Fairfax, just outside park boundaries, blossomed briefly; but today they are half abandoned and quiet, bypassed by the importance that gave them rise.

Rainfall is heavier at Carbon River than elsewhere in the park, producing a luxuriant forest. Western hemlock and Douglas-fir commonly measure three or four feet in diameter, and huge redcedar and occasional Sitka spruce intermix. Branches are draped with a lichen that looks like Spanish moss, but is actually not related. Devil's club and vine maple form a dense understory; lady fern and sword fern pad the forest floor, and fern moss grows on fallen trees and stumps.

The short nature trail just inside the park boundary winds through semi–rain forest identifying plants and explaining forest relationships. Notice the "wall" of roots formed by a windthrown Douglas-fir near the trail's end. Other short forest walks are to Green Lake and Chenuis Falls. (See Hiking chapter.)

The road ends at Ipsut Campground, 5 miles inside the park.

MOWICH LAKE, the largest lake in the park (one hundred acres), lies in a basin gouged by a glacier. The water is nearly two hundred feet deep, and exceptionally clear. Flowers bloom in the surrounding meadows through the summer—and are trampled into oblivion by the feet of humans who come to enjoy them. The Park Service is attempting to rebuild soil around the shore and thereby allow the meadow and huckleberry slopes to recover. Beyond the lake a trail leads along high, forested slopes to Spray Falls; another trail goes to Eunice Lake and Tolmie Peak. (See Hiking chapter.)

WEST SIDE ROAD (Map 6)

Points of Interest: The road begins 1 mile inside Nisqually Entrance and winds along the forested west side of the park, providing access to trailheads and offering a good chance to see wildlife.

Road: Crosses ridges and stream drainages; no steep grades. Dead-ends near Klapatche Point, 13 miles. Unpaved; often dusty in summer. No campgrounds or facilities. Closed by snow from late October to May or June.

Watch for signs of beaver in the alder flat of FISH CREEK, 3.5 miles after turning off the Nisqually road. They feed on the alder, eating the cambium layer of trees they have felled. Their teeth stay sharp because the back is faced with relatively soft dentine that wears away, leaving a self-renewing chisel edge of hard enamel. Devil's club is abundant along Fish Creek—a thorny plant with plate-size, maple-shaped leaves and brilliant red berries in summer.

From TAHOMA VISTA (a horseshoe bend and parking area 4 miles beyond Fish Creek) the rock face of Mount Wow shows plainly, laced with waterfalls in early summer and dotted with the dark green of trees wherever ledges provide toehold. *Wow* is an Indian word for mountain goat. The animals often browse the mountain's cliffs and are easy to see through binoculars. Occasionally a goat comes down from the heights to the roadside, or a dead one will melt from the snow banked at the base of Mount Wow, victim of winter avalanching. The Gobblers Knob Lookout shows from Tahoma Vista as a tiny cube atop the highest rock on the western skyline.

ROUND PASS, 4,000 feet, offers a view of Rainier with the ice of the Tahoma and Puyallup glaciers spilling in great jumbles. The LAKE GEORGE trail (1 mile) begins here, climbing a forested slope rather steeply at first, then leveling. (See Hiking chapter.)

Two short trails begin at St. Andrews Creek, the second river crossing after Round Pass. One is a ten-minute walk beside the mossy banks of the creek to Denman Falls; the other is a 2-mile trail that climbs to Klapatche Park. (See Hiking chapter.) Huckleberries are ripe along both trails from July into October—red ones, shiny purple ones, and powdery blue ones.

KLAPATCHE POINT, 13 miles from the beginning of the West Side Road, touches the park boundary and offers a vantage point overlooking commercial forestland with clear-cut patches served by mazes of roads. The sight offends the eye, but Douglas-fir reforestation requires opening the land to sunshine, and the method has been considered sound, providing small timber as well as large is utilized and slopes are replanted promptly. However, the practice is now severely criticized because of soil damage and erosion, especially on steep slopes. Certainly the views from Klapatche Point contrast the uses of land inside the park and outside of it. Beyond the forest the sheen—or smog—of Puget Sound shows on clear days, with the Olympic Mountains occasionally tracing a faint silhouette on the far horizon.

The West Side Road often is closed at Klapatche Point. If this is the case, walk a few steps down the road for the view of Mount Rainier and the North Puyallup amphitheater. Avalanches are frequent, high enough on the mountain to be no hazard but close enough to permit an onlooker to see and hear their fall—part of the unending sculpturing of Rainier that began even before the last eruption had finished building the cone.

West Side Road

Rappelling from Pinnacle Peak

HIKING AND CLIMBING

PARADISE (Map 1)

WILDFLOWER WALKS: Sample the meadows starting either in a generally northwest direction, toward Alta Vista, or more eastwardly, toward Edith Creek Basin. The flowers usually are equally showy (mid-July to September). The Edith Creek trail has less climbing than Alta Vista. Ranger-naturalists lead flower walks in summer; ask at the Paradise Visitor Center for times and routes.

GLACIER VISTA: The trail begins in the main Paradise flower meadow, then climbs to the heather slopes and out to the moraine of the Nisqually Glacier, giving hikers a clear, close view of the ice. It is easy walking although steadily uphill. Watch for grouse and ptarmigan. Snowbanks last into August most years. For the round trip allow 2 or 3 hours; 3 miles, total distance (or from 3 to 5 miles farther by continuing via the Skyline loop trail). For a shorter, easier, and less dramatic walk to a viewpoint above a glacier, try the Nisqually Vista trail. It begins just north of the visitor center, by the parking plaza; about half a mile, round trip.

PANORAMA POINT: The trail leads through meadows and heather to a rocky high point (6,800 feet) overlooking the Tatoosh Range, with the snow cones of Mount Adams, Mount Hood (near Portland, Oregon), and Mount St. Helens silhouetted against the southern horizon. Allow a half day; 4.2-mile loop trail (or an additional 1.5 miles by returning via Edith Creek Basin).

CAMP MUIR: This is an all-day trip to the high camp from which climbing parties start for the summit of Rainier. The trail starts out in flower fields, but is on snow much of the way—a 5-mile steady climb. Prepare adequately for bad weather, which can move in suddenly even on a sunny day; carry compass and map (and know how to use them) in case fog blows in. The hike is strenuous; the unfolding panorama magnificent. Side trips can be taken to the McClure Rock cleaver without special equipment or experience, and to the crevasses of the Cowlitz Glacier by experienced and equipped climbers who have registered with park rangers.

GLACIER CLIMBING: To feel ice underfoot and know the immensity of a glacier at first hand, join a guided party onto the Nisqually Glacier. (Concessioner service; make arrangements at the Paradise Visitor Center.

73

Paradise Ice Caves   Comet Falls

Also permissible for private parties that are equipped and competently led.) Climbing rope, ice ax, and crampons are necessary. They are included with the guide service, available for rent, or bring your own. With equipment and experienced leadership the venture is quite safe, and it is awesome to stand on the lip of a crevasse, peering one hundred feet into the blue-white depths of the glacier, and on occasion to hear the creaking and snapping of moving ice. Half-day trip.

ICE CAVES: Tubes melt beneath the Paradise Glacier as air flows in along the meltstream. The ice roofs of the tubes are usually so thin by late summer or early fall that daylight is refracted through them as a deep blue. No hand light is needed to see the entry portion of the caves, but to probe very far within (*which may be dangerous*) a gasoline lantern or a strong flashlight with fresh batteries is necessary. Watch for marmots and ptarmigan along the trail to the caves. No special equipment is needed, but wear boots or heavy shoes and step firmly while crossing snowbanks with steep outruns. Allow 3 or 4 hours round trip from Paradise; about 5 miles. Guided trips are available in summer (small fee). The later in the season the better, for this hike.

FARAWAY ROCK: Here is a pleasant walk out Mazama Ridge with only one steep portion. Flowers are lush in summer; the chances of seeing bear and deer are good; marmots are almost certain. At the end of the trail there is a sweeping view of the Tatoosh Range and Reflection Lakes. Allow three or four hours; 6 miles round trip with return either along Mazama Ridge or looping through Paradise Valley (about the same distance either way).

COMET FALLS AND VAN TRUMP PARK: The trail begins at Christine Falls on the Paradise road 4.5 miles above Longmire. Comet Falls leaps 320 feet in a free fall of foaming, roaring, splashing white. Van Trump Park is a high meadow carpeted with wildflowers from June through

September. Watch for pikas in the talus near Comet Falls and for mountain goats at Van Trump. For a dramatic view of the Kautz Creek flood damage (1947) walk to the ridge just west of Van Trump Park. Two and a half hours are enough for the falls round trip (only 1.5 miles each way); allow half a day—or a week—to explore Van Trump (a steep 0.8 mile beyond the falls).

STEVENS CANYON (Map 2)

PINNACLE PEAK: A steady climb, but short and worth it. The trail switchbacks up through huckleberry and fir on the north face of the Tatoosh Range and breaks into open talus country at a saddle just below Pinnacle Peak. Flowers are beautiful here, and the view is of Rainier with Gibraltar Rock jutting like an epaulet from the right-hand "shoulder." Listen for the high, thin call of pikas and the throatier shriek of marmots. The hike to the saddle is 1.3 miles by good trail from the Reflection Lake parking area; it is a considerable rock scramble from the saddle to the peak. Plan on two or three hours round trip, or a long half day with time for lunch and a nap in the sunshine at the saddle. Carry water if the day is hot.

BENCH AND SNOW LAKES: These two are such beautiful lakes, and the trail is so short, that it is a mistake to bypass them. Flowers, huckleberries, views of Rainier and of the Tatoosh Range, wildlife, birdsong, and lakes: few two-hour walks offer comparable delight. From the parking space beyond Lake Louise to Bench Lake is only 0.5 mile, and another 0.5 mile on to Snow Lake.

OHANAPECOSH (Map 3)

SILVER FALLS: The trail loops through a Douglas-fir and hemlock forest—a silent green world except for the singing of the river and the occasional chatter of a squirrel. Watch for elk, especially in autumn. The falls are a foaming cascade that can be reached by spur trails from the highway, although the 3-mile loop from Ohanapecosh gives the hiker time to savor more fully the forest setting. The loop trail starts near the Ohanapecosh Visitor Center; plan on about two hours for leisurely enjoyment, or take additional time and continue upriver to another waterfall about 6 miles farther. For a one-way hike, walk downriver from the Stevens Canyon Entrance Station, past Silver Falls, to Ohanapecosh; about 2 miles.

SHRINER PEAK: The trail starts in pleasant although unspectacular forest, then climbs through an old burn to open slopes that are often hot in summer. There is a fine view of Rainier and about the best chance in the park to see elk. A fire lookout tower tops the peak; hikers are permitted to climb to the catwalk and see the station. Carry water. The fire control aide manning the tower has to pack water for a mile, and thus cannot readily offer it to thirsty visitors. The climb is 4.2 miles, one way; allow most of a day.

TRAIL OF THE PATRIARCHS: This trail leads for 1 mile, round trip, through a grove of particularly large western redcedar, Douglas-fir, and western hemlock, some of the largest trees in the park. Allow about three quarters of an hour. The trail begins at the upper end of the parking lot beside Stevens Canyon Entrance Station; follow the East Side Trail a short way, then cross the river by a cable bridge and stroll in the silence of the ancient forest.

WHITE RIVER TO SUNRISE (Map 4)

WILDFLOWERS: Sample the Sourdough Mountain trail as far as time and energy warrant, or walk to Emmons Vista and then along the beginning of the main Burroughs Mountain trail, overlooking the valley of the White River.

EMMONS VISTA: Here is a quarter-mile walk to a spectacular vantage point with views up the Emmons and Winthrop glaciers and down the canyon of the White River. Allow twenty or thirty minutes to have time for noticing flowers along the way and for sensing the primordial grandeur of the scene at trail's end. The trail starts at the junction of the Lower Campground road near the Sunrise Visitor Center. The glacier exhibit and overlook are at the end of the lefthand trail. The righthand trail leads along the rim of the canyon toward Burroughs Mountain; ideal as a one-way, downhill hike to the campground or picnic area if transportation can be arranged.

THE BURROUGHS: The Burroughs is a high ridge coming off Mount Rainier in a series of three tundra-covered "humps." Go all the way to Third Burroughs, nearest the mountain, if time permits; 4 miles one way. No trail beyond Second Burroughs, but easy cross-country walking; follow the rock cairns and carry water. Watch for ptarmigan, rosy finches, horned larks, and pipits. Try this hike at dawn as light and sound flood the world anew. Allow at least half a day and preferably all day for the full hike.

FREMONT LOOKOUT: Walk west from the Sunrise Visitor Center across the broad slope of Sourdough Mountain, past Frozen Lake, where "icebergs" float until August, and on to the fire lookout (visitors permitted). No really steep climbing. Fine view of Rainier and the forested lowlands that stretch beyond the broad flat meadow of Grand Park. Open country all the way. Carry water. About 3 hours round trip; 2.5 miles each way.

SUMMERLAND: Flowers and access to high meadows make Summerland a favorite of hikers. The trail is a fairly steady forested climb beside Fryingpan Creek. Best as an all-day or overnight trip; 4.2 miles one way.

CARBON RIVER AND MOWICH LAKE (Map 5)

GREEN LAKE: This is a placid lake in a virgin forest setting. Be sure to take the short side trail to Ranger Falls, about halfway along the trail. Only 2 miles to the lake, but steep part way. Allow two hours, round trip.

CHENUIS FALLS: Cross the Carbon River by footlog and bridge and follow the trail into the forest to Chenuis Falls, which falls in sheets over dark gray rock and forms a limpid plunge pool. Water ouzels, chunky gray birds, often bob at the pool's edge and walk into the water to feed on insect larvae. The trail is level except for a last short, gentle pull to the falls; about 1.5 miles round trip. Allow three quarters of an hour. The crossing of the main Carbon River is down-river from the footbridge that spans the first small side channel.

CARBON GLACIER: The Carbon Glacier is the second largest in the park, after the Emmons—nearly four square miles of ice surface. Its headwall is the formidable Willis Wall. Climbers have reached the summit of Rainier via Curtis Ridge at the eastern rim of Willis Wall and via Ptarmigan and Liberty ridges to the west. Watch and listen for avalanches of ice thundering from the hanging glacier onto the Carbon Glacier. Rockfall is an extreme hazard at the snout of the glacier; *do not venture close.* The trail leaves from Ipsut Creek Campground; 4 miles to the glacier viewpoint. Allow three or four hours, round trip. Mystic Lake is 2.5 miles farther, ideal for an overnight hike late in the season when snow has melted.

TOLMIE PEAK: Hike west from Mowich Lake through high forest land to Ipsut Pass, then on past Eunice Lake to the fire lookout on Tolmie Peak. There is some climbing, but it alternates with easy going, and the lake alone is reward for the effort. Be there at sunset if possible and watch Rainier slip from the gleaming white of daytime into the pink and purple of alpine dusk, holding the sun's rays for an hour after they have left the meadows. To the lake is 2.5 miles (no overnight camping permitted); to Tolmie Peak is 0.8 miles farther (visitors are permitted to climb the tower). Allow about three hours hiking time to the peak, one way, plus at least an hour for enjoying the views.

SPRAY PARK: To find spring in August, hike to Spray Park. Avalanche lilies bloom at the edges of late-melting snowbanks, while lupine and elephanthead are maturing seed a few feet away. Plan an overnight stay if possible. About 5 to 6 miles, one way, depending on the campsite picked (no shelters). Be sure to take the 0.3-mile side trail to Spray Falls, about 3 miles from Mowich Lake.

WEST SIDE ROAD (Map 6)

INDIAN HENRYS HUNTING GROUND: An Indian chief named Satolick who lived below Eatonville used to hunt mountain goats here in the late nineteenth century. He was an excellent hunter, and he needed to be, according to early-day white settlers, for he had three wives to feed. The name "Henry" came from a chance meeting with James Longmire, William Packwood, and Henry Windsor in 1862 when the three were scouting a route through the Cascade Mountains. They asked Satolick his "Boston" name, and when he answered that he had none, Windsor said, "Take mine." Satolick did, and was known as Indian Henry from then on. His "hunting ground" is a luxuriant flower meadow with knolls to explore and a small gem lake that mirrors Point Success. For a close look onto an active part of the South Tahoma Glacier, walk above Indian Henrys toward Pyramid Peak. The sounds of falling rock and ice are continuous, and dust often plumes skyward as though it were steam heralding an eruption. Several trails lead to Indian Henrys; the most scenic begins at Tahoma Creek, 3.6 miles one way. The hike is comfortable as a one-day trip, or ideal as an overnight.

GOBBLERS KNOB: Here is a fine sunset hike. The climb requires persistence except for a short level stretch at Lake George (0.8 miles from the road), but there is drama in breaking out of the forest onto the bare crags around the lookout. Stay while the last sunlight glows on Mount Rainier and the lowlands slip into dusk. Carry water; the fire control aide has to pack his up. Visitors are permitted to climb the tower. Plan on an hour and a half going up to Gobblers Knob and forty-five minutes coming down (2.3 miles each way).

EMERALD RIDGE: To arrive at actively moving ice without leaving a forest and meadow trail, walk to the upper end of Emerald Ridge. Here the Tahoma Glacier pushes close against the ridge, and the ice is split by crevasses and pinnacled by seracs. Notice the sounds: the trickle of meltwater, the groan of moving ice, the occasional plop of mud dropping from an overhang. Mountain goats are frequent. If transportation can be arranged, this can be a loop hike, going up by the South Puyallup River trail and returning along Tahoma Creek. Emerald Ridge is at the midway point, about 4 miles from either trailhead. Watch for the andesite columns

Tahoma Glacier at Emerald Ridge

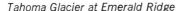

1.3 miles along the South Puyallup River trail (just off the trail to the right, going up, and easily missed). For a short hike the andesite is a worthwhile destination in itself. The Tahoma Creek trail leads along the moraine of the Tahoma Glacier part way, paralleling the wild, raw valley strewn with boulders and laced with silt-laden runoff from the ice.

KLAPATCHE PARK: A small pond dots the flower and heather meadow of the ridgetop here, and Rainier rises just beyond. The pond is filling in and turning to meadow, part of the natural process that makes alpine lakes among the most ephemeral of landscape features. The trail switchbacks to the ridge from St. Andrews Creek, then follows a fairly gentle slope to Klapatche Park, 2.5 miles one way. Plan on at least half a day; all day or overnight if possible. St. Andrews Park, 0.7 miles beyond Klapatche, is so high that it often stays under snow until August.

SUNSET PARK: A fire control aide stationed on the Sunset tower once entered in his official log: "There are 10,629 steps from here to the West Side Road"—and on hot August days hikers may feel his count was conservative. The trail sidehills through an old burn, then levels out in the high meadow country. Try the spur trail to Colonnades if time permits; it ends on a ridge with a particularly fine view of Rainier. Good chance to see goats. From Sunset Park, there are views both eastward to the mountain and westward to Puget Sound. A fifteen-minute walk below the lookout leads to the Golden Lakes, a dozen tarns; some have no trail but are easily reached by following a topographic map. From the end of the West Side Road to the lookout is 4.9 miles, or 3 miles additional if the road is closed at Klapatche Point.

WONDERLAND TRAIL (Map inside back cover)

A 90-mile trail circles Mount Rainier, crossing the ridges that radiate from the cone like spokes from a hub. The trail leads through silent forests, beside cascading streams, up huckleberry slopes, across flower meadows and snowbanks, to lakes and peaks and overlooks. Always there is the Mountain—Rainier with Point Success dominating the skyline; Rainier with awesome Willis Wall; Rainier with the Emmons and Winthrop glaciers spilling like frozen rivers from the summit. There are small shelter cabins every 6 to 10 miles—available to all comers and likely to be crowded on wet nights. The trail touches roads at Longmire, Mowich Lake, Ipsut Creek, Sunrise, White River, and Stevens Canyon, simplifying reprovisioning if arrangements can be made with friends. The entire loop takes about ten days, or the trail can be hiked in segments. Plan a leisurely trip with time to enjoy the full scene. It is a mistake to let the demand of "making miles" usurp the time to count varieties of flowers by the trailside, or to sit reveling in a breeze at the top of switchbacks and enjoying the sudden lightness of shoulders temporarily relieved of a pack.

Carry a warm sleeping bag (preferably down), a wool sweater, a raincoat or poncho, sun goggles, and tanning lotion; and wear boots. Menus can include special dehydrated trail foods available at outdoor recreation stores, or staples direct from the grocery store shelf such as cereal, packaged soups, quick-cooking macaroni and cheese, and instant rice with chipped beef or a small can of tuna added. Aluminum foil can be folded into a reflector oven for baking biscuits, or trout, by the fire. Good outdoor manners call for thoroughly burning refuse and packing back out used foil or plastic and empty cans—admittedly a nuisance but the most feasible way of sharing wilderness in these days of increasingly heavy use.

Plan to cross glacial rivers that have no bridge in the morning before melting of snow and ice swell them to midday force. Check with the National Park Service for current trail information. Carry maps.

THE SUMMIT CLIMB

The most commonly used routes to the summit of Rainier are from Paradise to Camp Muir and on via the Cowlitz Glacier to the Ingraham Glacier and Disappointment Cleaver. From White River the route is to Steamboat Prow and then up the Emmons Glacier. The usual schedule calls for high camp the first day, and on to the summit and all the way back down the second day. Necessary equipment includes rope, ice ax, and crampons (steel frameworks with spikes to grip the ice, worn on boot soles). All climbers going above the ten-thousand-foot level must either go with franchised guides or register with park rangers and be at least eighteen years old (or have written permission of parent or guardian). Solo climbing requires written permission from the park superintendent. Guide service and equipment are available from the concessioner, with summer headquarters at Paradise; ask about current fees and schedules. Good physical condition is requisite, and so is determination; but previous experience is not needed for guided parties, as a training session on basic techniques is available the day before these climbs.

Rainier is a short climb as world mountains go, but no trail eases the way as on most California and Colorado high peaks, and the altitude gain from the sea-level lowlands of Puget Sound to 14,410 feet affects climbers more than on other United States mountains outside Alaska. Reaching the summit entails forsaking a sleeping bag in the dark coldness of predawn, tying into a rope, and setting forth aware at first of little beyond the steep pitch, the yellow gleam of flashlights dancing across ice, and the faint pulling and slackening of the rope as others vary pace. Parties usually leave high camp by 1:00 A.M. to allow time to get up and back before the heat of day loosens rocks held by ice and weakens snow bridges spanning crevasses. The distance to the summit is only 5 or 6 miles, but the way is steep, the air thin, and the route roughened with abrupt cleavers to climb and crevasses to thread between and occasionally jump across.

The high world of ice and rock and sky holds a beauty all its own, and the only way to know that beauty is to climb into it. There is new day catching the upper lip of a crevasse while the lower lip holds the blackness of night; and new day turning the ice underfoot to orange or rose, then at last flooding across the mountain with full white brilliance and the promise of warmth. There are pinnacles of ice, canyons of ice, ice crunching beneath crampons, ice easing thirst. There are days when the Puget Sound country lies below like a black-green carpet, covered with trees and set with cities that dot the wilderness with twentieth-century mankind. And there are days when clouds blanket the world with white cotton, and only Rainier and her sister volcanoes soar clear.

Above Little Tahoma

DIRECTORY

LODGING

INSIDE THE PARK

Paradise Inn : Open mid-June through Labor Day. For reservations write Mount Rainier Hospitality Services, Box 1136, Tacoma, Washington 98400.

Longmire Inn: Open early May to mid-October. Operated by the same company as above.

NEAR THE PARK

Cabins and lodges on the Paradise, Ohanapecosh, and White River approach roads; at Crystal Mountain and White Pass; in the communities of Eatonville, Morton, Packwood, and Enumclaw.

MEAL SERVICE

INSIDE THE PARK

Summer: Longmire Inn, Paradise Inn, Paradise Cafeteria (in visitor center), Sunrise (fountain services and snacks only).

Out of Season: Longmire Inn (snacks and coffee), Paradise Cafeteria (in the visitor center; open weekends and holidays only during ski season).

NEAR THE PARK

Year-round: Resort restaurants outside the park on the Paradise and White River roads; at Crystal Mountain and White Pass; and in the surrounding communities of Eatonville, Morton, Packwood, and Enumclaw.

CAMPGROUNDS

Check for latest information regarding limits, fees, and so on. Greatly increased use in all national parks is forcing change. Trailers and recreation vehicles are permitted in the campgrounds, but there are no hookups. White gas usually is available at Sunrise in summer and at Longmire all year, as well as at service stations outside the park. Presto logs often are available at the same locations.

NISQUALLY TO PARADISE (Map 1)

Sunshine Point: In an alder flat along the Nisqually River, 0.5 mile inside the park. 22 sites; pit toilets; piped water. Open all year except for occasional heavy snow. Elevation 2,000 feet.

Ohanapecosh Campground

Longmire: Among trees along the Nisqually River with view to Mount Rainier. 207 sites; flush toilets. Usually open in May while Cougar Rock Campground is still under snow, then used only as overflow. Elevation 2,750 feet.

Cougar Rock: On the Paradise road 2 miles above Longmire, among Douglas-fir and hemlock. 5 group sites, 183 regular sites, pull-through trailer sites; flush toilets. Open June to mid-October. Elevation 3,180 feet.

Paradise: Directly beneath the peak of Rainier in a setting of flowers and subalpine fir. 65 sites; flush toilets. Open mid-July (or whenever the snow melts) through September. Elevation 5,300 feet.

OHANAPECOSH (Map 3)

Ohanapecosh: Probably the most beautiful lowland campground in the park, set in virgin forest along the river. 234 sites; flush toilets. Open mid-May to late October. Elevation 1,914 feet.

WHITE RIVER TO SUNRISE (Map 4)

White River: Reached by dirt road turning along the White River 5 miles beyond the entrance station. Forested river bank. 120 sites; flush toilets. Open late June through mid-October. Elevation 4,400 feet.

Sunrise: Reached by a dirt road 1.5 miles below the Visitor Center; traditionally with separate areas for tents and recreation vehicles. Perhaps the most spectacular motor camp in the park, with flower meadows and views of Rainier close by. However, subalpine meadows are the most fragile zone in the park, and the heavy use they now receive may force closure of this campground, at least for rest periods. Check status. Elevation 6,500 feet.

CARBON RIVER AND MOWICH LAKE (Map 5)

Ipsut Creek: 5 miles inside the Carbon River entrance of the park; deep forest setting. 2 group sites and 28 regular sites; pit toilets; piped water. Open May through October. Elevation 2,500 feet.

Mowich Lake: On a ridge coming off the cone of Rainier; subalpine fir and flowers. Reached by a steep dirt road that turns 6.3 miles out of Wilkeson, and soon may be dead-ended after about 15 miles, leaving a 2- or 3-mile walk to the lake. Camping permitted at road's end; pit toilets. The lake itself has been closed to camping because of damage to fragile meadow plants. The same problem may prompt shortening of the road, whereby overuse will be avoided, leaving this particular lake for hikers and backpackers. Road closed by snow October to July. Lake elevation 4,929 feet.

WEST SIDE ROAD (Map 6)

Tahoma Creek: The small campground here has been repeatedly damaged by mudflows coming off the Tahoma Glacier and has had to be closed as unsafe. It serves now only as a parking area for trail access along Tahoma Creek. No motor campground is available out the West Side Road.

APPROACHES TO THE PARK

Nisqually-Paradise Approach Road (State 706): Alder Lake, a lakeside camp in the forest developed by the Tacoma City Light Company. Open all year. The lake is warm enough for swimming in summer. Elevation about 1,800 feet. Also Big Creek Camp along the Nisqually River outside the park, reached via Skate Creek Road. Open all year except when blocked by snow. Elevation about 2,000 feet.

Packwood to Ohanapecosh (US 12): River Bar and La Wis Wis, on the Cowlitz River in forest settings; National Forest land. Open all year. Elevation about 1,500 feet.

White Pass (US 12): Summit Creek and Soda Springs reached by turning off the highway onto National Forest road No. 1400 (unpaved). Mountain settings; minimum development. These are jump-off points for high-country hiking. Open July to October. Elevation about 2,800 feet.

Chinook Pass (State 410): American Forks, Pine Needle, Hell's Crossing, Pleasant Valley, Lodgepole, Morse Creek, and others on the east slope of the Cascades; see Sources of Information for Forest Service offices to write for complete lists. Elevations from about 2,800 to 4,000 feet. Some campgrounds are open all year, others through the warm season only.

White River Approach Road (State 410): The Dalles and Silver Springs, National Forest campgrounds southeast of Enumclaw; forested river bank settings. Open all year except when blocked by snow. Elevations 2,165 and 2,650 feet. Also Weyerhaeuser Company public camps (free) located at Twin Creeks and Greenwater River parks, off State 410 east of Enumclaw. Open all year; elevation about 1,800 feet.

PICNIC AREAS

All campgrounds are open for picnicking. In the park there are special picnic areas at the approach to the Nisqually Bridge, at Paradise, at Box Canyon on the Stevens Canyon Road (shaded; view to Mount Adams), and at Sunrise. A riverside area across from Cougar Rock Campground is for picnicking; sometimes Longmire Campground is open for this use. On the Paradise approach to the park there is a forested State Highway Department rest area 2 miles west of Ashford. On the White Pass approach, the Palisade picnic area offers a view of Rainier, plus a geologic display, and there is a small walk-in area at Kuppenberg Lake. Along US 410 north of White River, there are small picnic areas at Dry Creek and at Federation Forest State Park.

PUBLIC TRANSPORTATION

Mount Rainier Hospitality Services in Tacoma and Western Tours in Seattle operate bus service to Mount Rainier, suitable as a one-day sightseeing tour (216 miles round trip from Seattle) or as transportation to the park with a later return. Write for current schedule and rates.

SUPPLIES AND SERVICES

Gasoline (year-round unless otherwise noted): Gateway Inn at Nisqually Entrance (often closed part of the winter), Longmire, Sunrise (summer only), Silver Springs near White River Entrance, and Greenwater, 15 miles north of the entrance; surrounding communities of Eatonville, Elbe, Ashford, Morton, Packwood, Enumclaw, and Wilkeson.

Groceries: Same locations as gasoline. Very limited selection within the park and immediately adjoining; complete selection in the surrounding communities.

Showers: Concession at Longmire.

Laundry: None in the park; coin-operated laundries in Eatonville, Morton, Packwood, and Enumclaw.

Ice: Available inside the park at Sunrise (summer only); also outside the park at Eatonville, Ashford, Morton, Packwood, Enumclaw, and Wilkeson.

Post Office: Longmire (all year), Paradise (summer only); also Eatonville, Elbe, Ashford, Morton, Packwood, Enumclaw, Wilkeson, and Carbonado.

Medical Service: Clinic at Eatonville; hospital at Morton; hospital in Enumclaw. Sometimes a nurse at Paradise; emergency first aid at any ranger station.

Telephones: Longmire, Paradise, Ohanapecosh, White River Ranger Station and Campground, Sunrise (summer only); all surrounding communities; any ranger station in an emergency (radio contact with headquarters at Longmire).

FISHING

Four species of trout are found in the lakes: Eastern brook (which is actually a charr), rainbow, cutthroat, sockeye salmon (a land-locked Kokanee). These same four plus Dolly Varden are in the streams and rivers.

No license is required to fish park waters; regulations follow those of the state with some additional restrictions. Check for the current specifics. Closed waters include Reflection, Tipsoo, Shadow, and Frozen lakes; also Laughingwater, Klickitat, and Ipsut creeks above the water intakes.

The best streams generally are the Paradise River (good from August to September) and the Ohanapecosh River (all summer for medium or better fly fishermen). Glacial rivers—the Carbon, Nisqually, White, and others—usually are best early in the season while glacial flour is at a minimum. Streams are not stocked with fish; lakes are, and they therefore vary from year to year depending on the stocking program. Many lakes are exceptionally clear and for best results should be fished with a light line.

Fishing the Nisqually River

NATURALIST SERVICES AND FACILITIES

Nature Trails: Kautz Mudflow (Paradise road), Trail of the Shadows (Long-mire), Ice Caves (Paradise), Trail of the Patriarchs (Ohanapecosh), Emmons Vista and Sourdough Ridge (Sunrise), Forest (Carbon River).

Naturalist-led Walks (summer only): Usually Longmire, Paradise, Ohanape-cosh, Sunrise, White River, and Ipsut Creek.

Illustrated Talks (summer only): Usually at Longmire Community Building (in the old campground), Paradise Visitor Center, Ohanapecosh Amphitheater, Sunrise Visitor Center, White River Campground, and Ipsut Creek (Carbon River). Check current schedule.

GUIDE SERVICE

The services offered vary from year to year; write for specific information (see Sources of Information for address) or check at the Paradise Visitor Center. Typical guided trips include one-day ice climbing (a beginners' session required of inexperienced summit climbers, and an advanced session for those already familiar with basic techniques); the two-day summit climb; rock climbing and conducted trips to the Ice Caves or into the Tatoosh Range. Also high-country seminars in photography, mountaineering medicine, and expeditions; generally five-day sessions with base camp at the 10,000-foot level of the mountain. Ski lessons sometimes available in summer, on request. No guided saddle trips because of the severe trail erosion caused by horses.

WINTER ACTIVITY

The Paradise road is open daily except during heavy storms; skiing (rope tows), snowshoeing, and sledding from December to May. Ski equipment and sleds for rent at Paradise. Ski instruction; guided tours to Camp Muir, subject to demand and weather conditions. Meal service at Paradise on weekends and holidays; no overnight accommodations.

Crystal Mountain, outside the park near White River, has complete ski resort facilities including a chair lift; so does White Pass, near Ohanapecosh. The lifts are worth riding for the view even for nonskiers, but wear warm clothes and carry blankets.

SOURCES OF INFORMATION

Superintendent, Mount Rainier National Park, Longmire, Washington 98397. Year-round ranger stations in the park: Nisqually, Longmire, Ohanapecosh, White River.

Mount Rainier Hospitality Services, Government Services, Inc., Box 1136, Tacoma, Washington 98400 (for lodging information and reservations).

Rainier Guide Service, Mount Rainier National Park, Paradise, Washington 98398.

Gifford Pinchot National Forest, District Ranger, Packwood, Washington 98361 (for information on National Forest land adjoining the park on the southeast).

Snoqualmie National Forest, District Ranger, 1415 Blake Street, Enumclaw, Washington 98022 (for information on National Forest land adjoining the park primarily on the east and north).

READING LIST

CAHALANE, VICTOR H. *Mammals of North America.* New York: Macmillan & Co., 1943. Informative and enjoyable account of mammals, including Mount Rainier species.

CRANDELL, D. R. *The Geologic Story of Mount Rainier.* Washington, D.C.: U.S. Geological Survey Bulletin No. 1292, 1969. Readable and authoritative look at the mountain's geologic past.

―――, and D. R. MULLINEAUX. *Volcanic Hazards of Mount Rainier.* Washington, D.C.: U.S. Geological Survey Bulletin No. 1238, 1967. Discusses Rainier as a volcano today, compared with its past.

FISKE, RICHARD S., CLIFFORD A. HOPSON, and AARON C. WATERS. *Geology of Mount Rainier National Park.* Washington, D.C.: U.S. Geological Survey Professional Paper No. 444, 1963. Technical treatise.

FRIES, MARY A. with photos by BOB and IRA SPRING. *Wildflowers of Mount Rainier and the Cascades.* Seattle: Mount Rainier Natural History Association and The Mountaineers, 1970. Informative, brief descriptions; color photographs.

HAINES, AUBREY L. *Mountain Fever.* Portland: Oregon Historical Society, 1962. Story of the exploration and early ascents of Mount Rainier, to about 1900.

LARRISON, EARL J., and KLAUS G. SONNENBERG. *Washington Birds: Their Location and Identification.* Seattle: Audubon Society, 1968. Descriptions of species with notes on behavior and ecology; drawings.

LYONS, C. P. *Trees, Shrubs and Flowers to Know in Washington.* Revised ed. Vancouver, B.C.: J. M. Dent & Sons, 1967. Excellent field identification guide; drawings and descriptions.

MANNING, HARVEY (ed.). *Mountaineering: The Freedom of the Hills.* Seattle: Mountaineers, 1960. Comprehensive résumé of wilderness hiking, camping, and climbing.

MCKENNY, MARGARET, revised and enlarged by DANIEL R. STUNTZ. *The Savory Wild Mushroom.* Seattle and London: University of Washington Press, 1971. Introduction to mushrooms, helpful in identification and cookery.

MOLENAAR, DEE. *Pictorial Relief Map.* 1965; available from Mount Rainier Natural History Association, Longmire, Wash. Clear presentation of Rainier topography, detailing glaciers, ridges, roads, and trails.

―――. *The Challenge of Rainier.* Seattle: Mountaineers, 1971. Detailed history of climbs: the men and the mountain. Drawings and photographs.

SPRING, IRA, and HARVEY MANNING. *50 Hikes in Mount Rainier National Park.* Seattle: Mount Rainier Natural History Association and The Mountaineers, 1969. Photos, text, and map detailing fifty favorite hikes in the park.

INDEX

MAP 2 JOINS HERE

Ohanapecosh 23 mi.
from Paradise

Paradise Gl.
Ice caves
Snow L.
0.5   0.5
Bench L.
Louise L.
Panorama Pt
Faraway Rock
Reflection L.
Nisqually Gl.
PARADISE 5400
Pinnacle Pk 6562
1.3
Narada Falls
13
Van Trump Park
Comet Falls
1.5
Christine Falls
Paradise R.
TATOOSH
RANGE
Ricksecker Pt
Eagle Pk 5955
COUGAR ROCK
3.5
Nisqually R.
Rampart Ridge
Kautz Cr.
LONGMIRE 2762
3
Mudflow Exhibit
Tahoma Cr.
West Side Road (closed in winter)
Skate Creek Road (closed in winter)
Nisqually R.
2
1
SUNSHINE POINT
NISQUALLY ENTRANCE 2000
Tacoma 56 mi.
Seattle 80 mi.
N MILE

MAP 6 JOINS HERE

Klapatche Park
Puyallup Gl.
Tahoma
S. Puyallup R.
EMERALD RIDGE
Tahoma Gl.
Tumtum Pk
Kautz
Nisqually R.

Ranger station
Visitor center (museum)
Campground
Picnic only
Fire lookout
Trail and shelter ⋯ 2.4 ▲⋯
Road ⋅ 3.2 ⋅ 4.0
surfaced   graveled
(mileage between points)

MAP 1

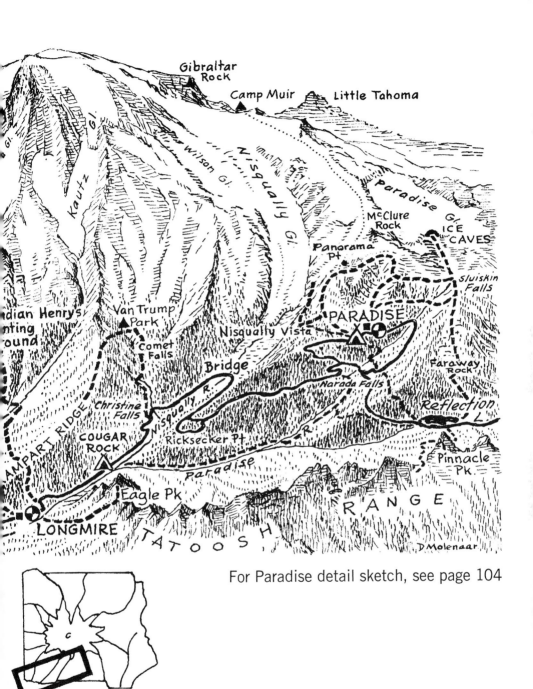

Gibraltar
Rock

Camp Muir   Little Tahoma

Kautz Gl.

Wilson Gl.

Nisqually Gl.

Paradise Gl.

McClure
Rock

ICE
CAVES

Panorama
Pt.

Sluiskin
Falls

dian Henry's
nting
ound

Van Trump
Park

Comet
Falls

Nisqually Vista

PARADISE

Faraway
Rock

Bridge

Narada Falls

Reflection
L.

Nisqually R.

Christine
Falls

RAMPART RIDGE

COUGAR
ROCK

Ricksecker Pt.

Paradise R.

Pinnacle
Pk.

Eagle Pk

R A N G E

LONGMIRE

T A T O O S H

D. Molenaar

For Paradise detail sketch, see page 104

Nisqually to Paradise

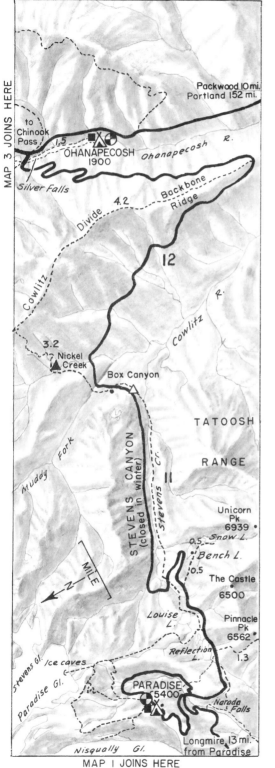

MAP 3 JOINS HERE

Packwood 10 mi.
Portland 152 mi.

to
Chinook
Pass

.5

OHANAPECOSH
1900

Ohanapecosh R.

Silver Falls

Divide

4.2

Backbone
Ridge

Cowlitz

12

Cowlitz R.

3.2

Nickel
Creek

Box Canyon

Muddy Fork

STEVENS CANYON
(closed in winter)

Stevens Cr.

TATOOSH

RANGE

Unicorn
Pk
6939

0.5 Snow L.

Bench L.

0.5

The Castle
6500

Louise
L.

Pinnacle
Pk
6562

Reflection
L.

1.3

MILE

N

Stevens Gl. Ice caves

Paradise Gl.

PARADISE
5400

Narada
Falls

Longmire, 13 mi.
from Paradise

Nisqually Gl.

MAP I JOINS HERE

Wilson Gl.

PARADISE

MAZAMA RIDGE

Reflection
L.

Unicorn
Pk

TATOOSH

RANGE

Stevens Cr.

D. Molenaar

Ranger station
Visitor center (museum)
Campground
Picnic only
Fire lookout
Trail and shelter   2.4
Road   3.2   4.0

surfaced   graveled
(mileage between points)

MAP 2

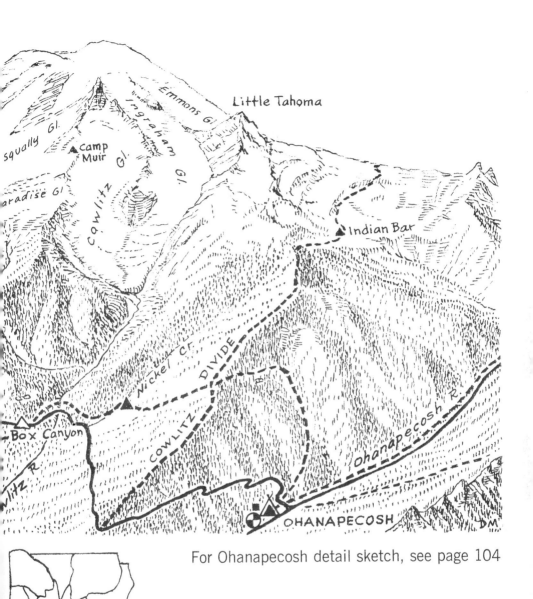

Little Tahoma

Emmons Gl.

Ingraham Gl.

squally Gl.

Camp Muir

Cowlitz Gl.

aradise Gl.

Paradise Gl.

Indian Bar

Nickel Cr.

DIVIDE

COWLITZ

Ohanapecosh R.

Box Canyon

litz R.

OHANAPECOSH

DM

For Ohanapecosh detail sketch, see page 104

Stevens Canyon

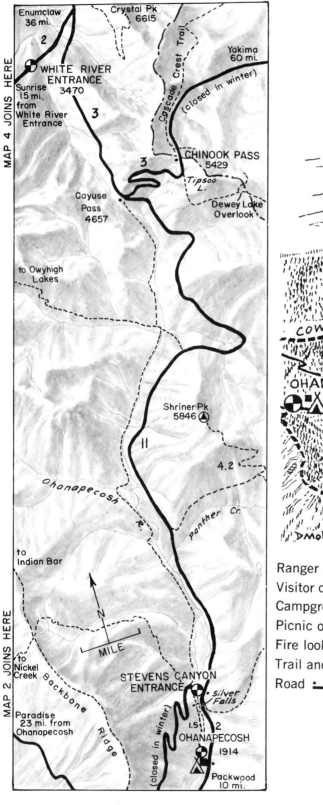

MAP 4 JOINS HERE

Enumclaw
36 mi.

Crystal Pk
6615

2

Yakima
60 mi.

WHITE RIVER
ENTRANCE
3470

Cascade Crest Trail

(closed in winter)

Sunrise
15 mi.
from
White River
Entrance

3

CHINOOK PASS
5429

3

Tipsoo
L.

Cayuse
Pass
4657

Dewey Lake
Overlook

to Owyhigh
Lakes

Shriner Pk.
5846

II

4.2

Ohanapecosh
R.

Panther Cr.

to
Indian Bar

N

MILE

MAP 2 JOINS HERE

to
Nickel
Creek

Backbone

Ridge

Paradise
23 mi. from
Ohanapecosh

STEVENS CANYON
ENTRANCE

Silver
Falls

(closed in winter)

1.5

2

OHANAPECOSH
1914

Packwood
10 mi.

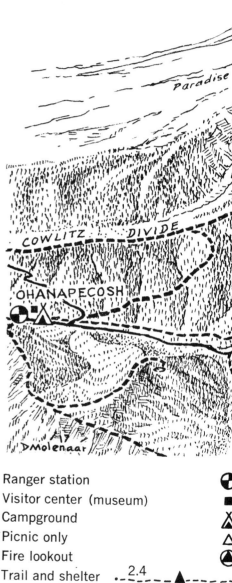

Paradise

COWLITZ DIVIDE

OHANAPECOSH

D.Molenaar

Ranger station

Visitor center (museum)

Campground

Picnic only

Fire lookout

Trail and shelter   2.4

Road   3.2   4.0

surfaced   graveled
(mileage between points)

MAP 3

Little
Tahoma

Winthrop Gl.

Emmons Gl.

Ingraham Gl.

Gl.

itz Gl.

pr

Summerland

Indian
Bar

Cowlitz Chimneys

Fryingpan Cr.

Ohanapecosh R.

White R.

SUNRISE

WHITE
RIVER
ENTRANCE

Cayuse Pass

riner

CHINOOK PASS

Tipsoo L.

To Yakima

Ohanapecosh to Chinook Pass

MAP 5 JOINS HERE

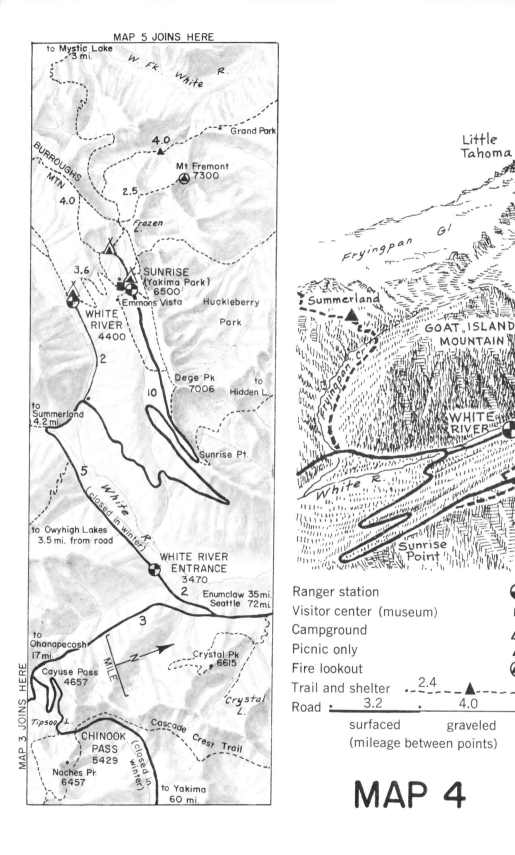

to Mystic Lake
3 mi.

W. FK. White R.

Grand Park

4.0

Mt Fremont
7300

2.5

BURROUGHS MTN

4.0

Frozen

3.6

SUNRISE
(Yakima Park)
6500

Emmons Vista

Huckleberry

WHITE
RIVER
4400

Park

2

Dege Pk
7006

to
Hidden L.

10

to
Summerland
4.2 mi.

5

White R. (closed in winter)

Sunrise Pt.

to Owyhigh Lakes
3.5 mi. from road

WHITE RIVER
ENTRANCE
3470

2   Enumclaw 35 mi.
Seattle 72 mi.

3

to
Ohanapecosh
17 mi.

MILE

Crystal Pk
6615

Cayuse Pass
4657

Crystal L.

Tipsoo L.

Cascade Crest Trail

CHINOOK
PASS
5429 (closed in winter)

Naches Pk
6457

to Yakima
60 mi.

MAP 3 JOINS HERE

Little
Tahoma

Fryingpan Gl

Summerland

GOAT ISLAND
MOUNTAIN

Fryingpan Cr.

WHITE
RIVER

White R.

Sunrise
Point

Ranger station

Visitor center (museum)

Campground

Picnic only

Fire lookout

Trail and shelter   2.4

Road   3.2   4.0

surfaced   graveled
(mileage between points)

MAP 4

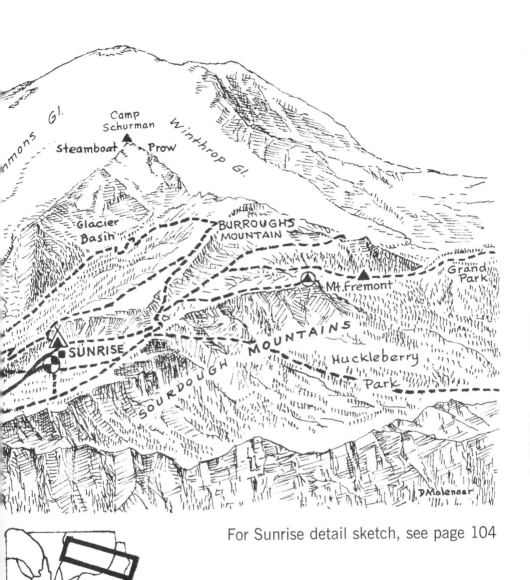

Camp
Schurman

Steamboat Prow

mons Gl.

Winthrop Gl.

Glacier
Basin

BURROUGHS
MOUNTAIN

Mt. Fremont

Grand
Park

SUNRISE

SOURDOUGH   MOUNTAINS

Huckleberry
Park

D.Molenaar

For Sunrise detail sketch, see page 104

White River to Sunrise

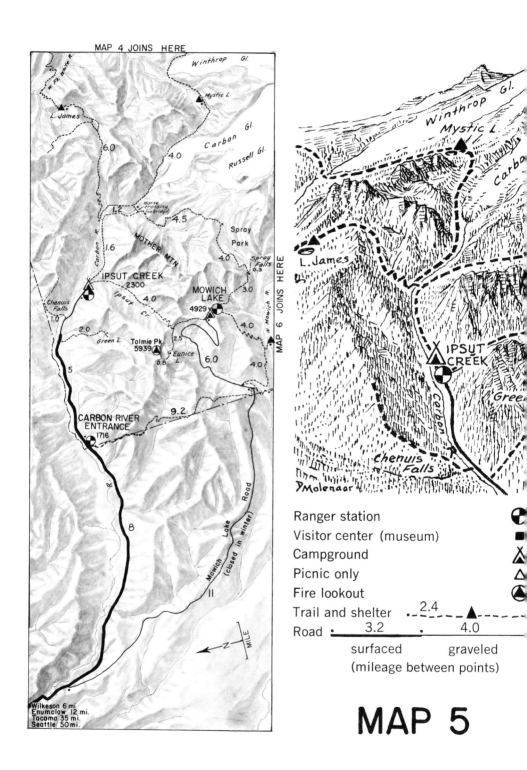

MAP 4 JOINS HERE

Winthrop Gl.

Mystic L.

W. Fk. White R.

L. James

6.0

4.0

Carbon Gl.

Russell Gl.

1.2

Horse crossing (no bridge)

4.5

MOTHER MTN.

1.6

Spray Park

4.0

Spray Falls
0.3

IPSUT CREEK
2300

Carbon R.

Ipsut Cr.

4.0

MOWICH LAKE
4929

3.0

Chenuis Falls

1.0

2.0

Green L.

Tolmie Pk
5939

2.5

Eunice L.
0.8

6.0

N. Mowich R.

4.0

4.0

5

CARBON RIVER
ENTRANCE
1716

9.2

MAP 6 JOINS HERE

R.

8

Mowich Lake Road (closed in winter)

11

N

MILE

Winthrop Gl.

Mystic L.

Carbo

L. James

IPSUT CREEK

Green

Chenuis Falls

D. Molenaar

Ranger station

Visitor center (museum)

Campground

Picnic only

Fire lookout

Trail and shelter   2.4

Road   3.2   4.0

surfaced   graveled

(mileage between points)

MAP 5

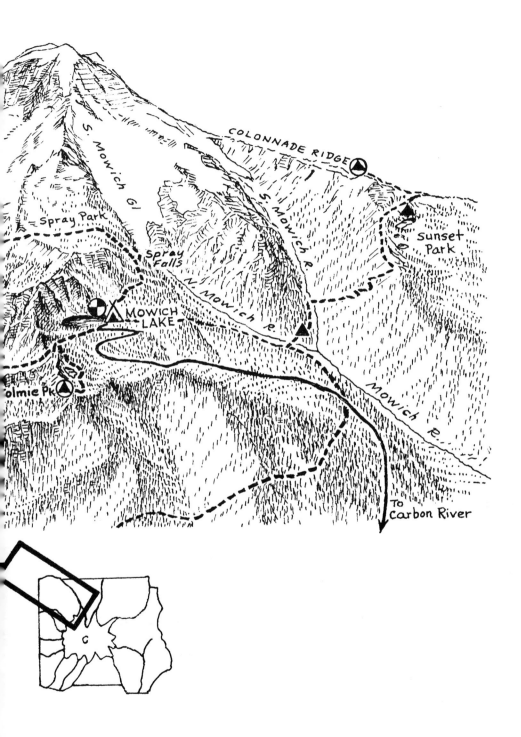

Carbon River and Mowich Lake

MAP 5 JOINS HERE

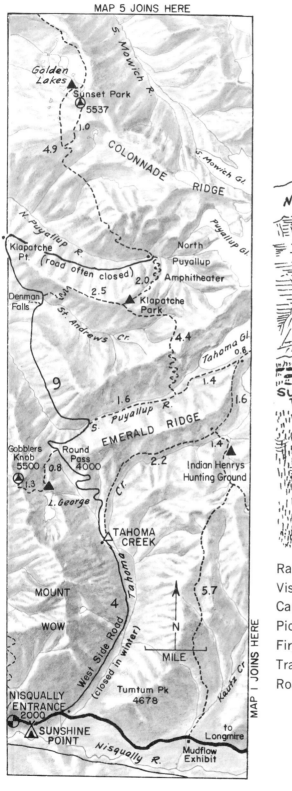

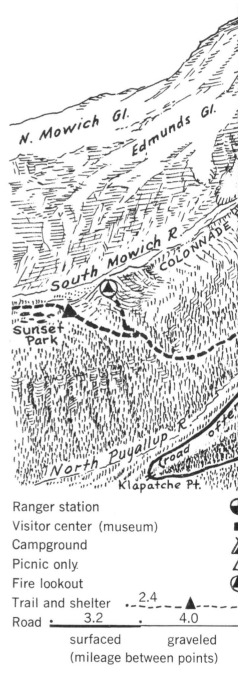

Ranger station
Visitor center (museum)
Campground
Picnic only
Fire lookout
Trail and shelter ●----- 2.4 -----▲
Road ●——— 3.2 ———●———— 4.0 ————
surfaced   graveled
(mileage between points)

MAP 6

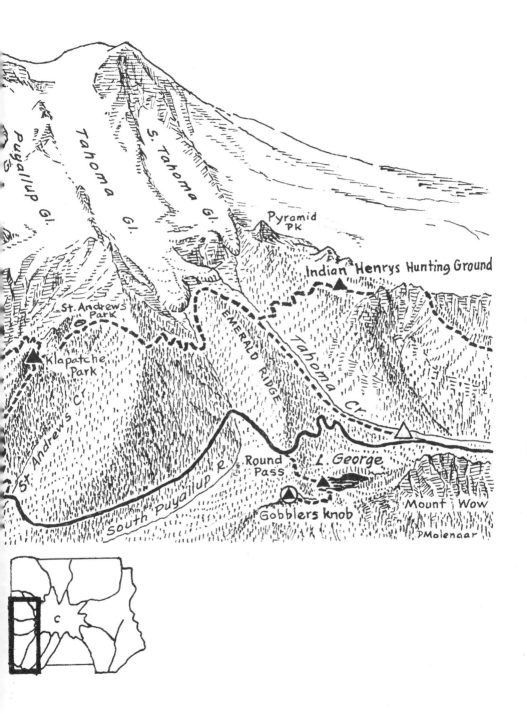

Pugallup Gl.

Tahoma Gl.

S. Tahoma Gl.

S. Tahoma Gl.

Pyramid Pk

Indian Henrys Hunting Ground

St. Andrews Park

EMERALD RIDGE

Tahoma Cr.

Klapatche Park

St. Andrews Cr.

St.

South Puyallup R.

Round Pass

L. George

Gobblers knob

Mount Wow

D.Molenaar

c

West Side Road

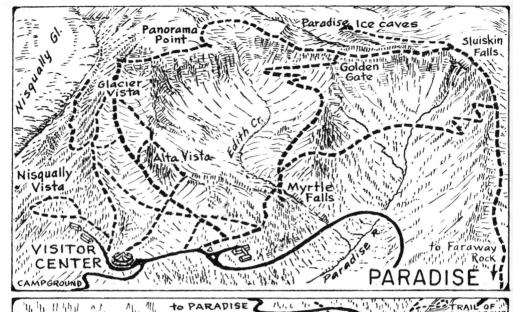

PARADISE

Nisqually Gl.
Panorama Point
Paradise Ice caves
Sluiskin Falls
Golden Gate
Glacier Vista
Edith Cr.
Alta Vista
Nisqually Vista
Myrtle Falls
VISITOR CENTER
Paradise R.
to Faraway Rock
CAMPGROUND

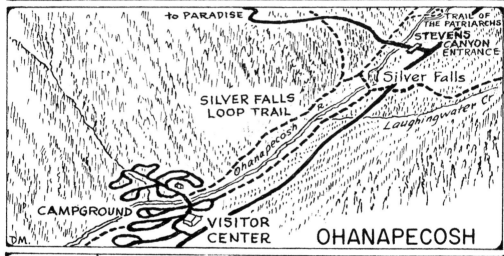

OHANAPECOSH

to PARADISE
TRAIL OF THE PATRIARCHS
STEVENS CANYON ENTRANCE
Silver Falls
SILVER FALLS LOOP TRAIL
Laughingwater Cr.
Ohanapecosh R.
CAMPGROUND
VISITOR CENTER
D.M.

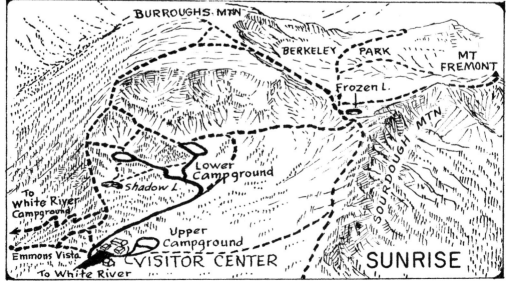

SUNRISE

BURROUGHS MTN
BERKELEY PARK
MT FREMONT
Frozen L.
SOURDOUGH MTN
Lower Campground
Shadow L.
To White River Campground
Upper Campground
Emmons Vista
VISITOR CENTER
To White River